A. Renee Wilson

Man~Kation
®

A vacation from dating *Men* and preparing for the *Man* God has for you!

Perfecting Proverbs
Publishing

Man-kation

Copyright © 2013 by A. Renee Wilson. All rights reserved. In accordance with the U.S. Copyright Act of 1976, the scanning, uploading, and electronic sharing of any part of this book without the publisher or author's permission is unlawful piracy and theft of the author's property. Thank you for supporting the author's rights.

All scripture is taken from the King James Bible and the Amplified Bible.

Published in the United States of America

Revised Version

Dedication

In loving memory of my father, Larry Wilson, and my grandfather, James Sheard, Sr. Both men played a tremendous part in the woman that I am today. I reflected on the times I spent with each of them throughout the process of writing this book, and it helped me to appreciate God's grace of having them in my life.

To my daddy: I thank you for being the first man in my life to show me what love is. You taught me how a man should respect, treat, and cherish me. We had a friendship and a closeness that I will never forget. Though you were tall and strong and served our country in the Navy during the Vietnam War very well, underneath, you were the giant teddy bear that I always found comfort in. I can't wait to see you again to rest in your arms and dance with you!

To my papa: Wow! I have so much love and gratitude for you! You also served our country in two wars, WWII, and the Korean conflict. You were a decorated soldier. You and grandma managed to raise a family of eight children (five boys & three girls) successfully. I thank you for always teaching me the word of God and singing hymns to me. You never let the word of God depart from your mouth. I have so many memories of the example you set for me to be a student of the Word. I thank you for your prayers and know that the seeds you sowed are being reaped by your children. When I see you in heaven, I can't wait to hear you say; "You kept God first, Papa's baby!"

Contents

	Introduction
Chapter 1:	What is a Man~kation?
Chapter 2:	The "Wilderness Man" Search
Chapter 3:	How a Man~kation Can Heal Your Broken Heart?
Chapter 4:	Avoid the Tricks of the Enemy
Chapter 5:	Walk in Wisdom
Chapter 6:	Love is a Characteristic Not just an Emotion
Chapter 7:	The Schizophrenic Soul
Chapter 8:	Killing your Ego
Chapter 9:	Leave your baggage in the Wilderness
Chapter 10:	Enter God's Garden by Faith
Chapter 11:	If You Want a Boaz You Must Be a Ruth
Chapter 12:	Pursue Your Purpose
Chapter 13:	The NEW YOU!
	A Word of Thanks!
	Meet the Author!
	To My Boaz

Introduction

Being single can be very difficult due to the dating that must be done to find that special person. Let's face it, dating is work—it's a lot of work! You must decide who to call, who to date, who to trust and so on. These questions can cause a lot of uncertainty, which makes us live in the never-ending cycle of an "emotional rollercoaster"! It's like being in a wilderness with no sense of direction.

Taking a vacation (a Man~kation) from all the work that "wilderness" dating requires is exactly what we need to regroup and renew ourselves. So, when we do return to dating, the work will be less strenuous because of the wisdom and strength we received from God.

God gave me the vision for this book to help my sisters in Christ get free from the "wilderness search" for a man. He said to me, "I want my daughters back!" Living in the chaotic wilderness separates us from God, because He is *not* the author of confusion (1 Corinthians 14:33). This disconnection from God doesn't allow us to reap the abundant life that Jesus promised (John 10:10).

There is a *process* to attain the abundant life and work that must be done on our part to receive the overflow from God, but we must be ready to change. Many people think that all they need to do is ask God for what they want, and like a genie He will make it appear. There are no *shortcuts* with God; the process is necessary to build endurance, character, and your relationship with Him!

I challenge you to take each chapter of this book and ask yourself: How does this relate to my past or current experiences? And how can this information help me?

I must warn you that this book is *not* for the women who "social date" to have fun. It's for the women that are *serious* about settling down and being ready for the special man *God* has for them! There's nothing worse than getting something you're not prepared for; you will be overwhelmed with the lack of *wisdom* it takes to keep it and end up losing it.

This Man~kation is for the *"serious vacationer"*, not the *overnighter* or the *weekender*, but for the women that are willing to go the long distance (whatever it takes) to get prepared! The *rewards* at the end of this journey will be well worth the time and energy you have invested. The new you and your "Prince Charming" are waiting, so let the adventure begin!

Chapter 1

What is Man-kation?

Man-kation is defined as a moment in time to break away from the focus of finding an earthly man to seeking God along the journey of preparing for our "destiny man"! A good friend told me that she was on a "vacation" from men…a "Man-kation". She talked about being tired of dating men, with no success in finding *her man!* I realized that I agreed with her completely and immediately knew that I felt the same way. I felt this way because I kept running into *the foolish man, the cheating man, the conceited man, the lustful man, the deceitful man,* and the *just plain old scandalous man!* I'm talking about men in and out of the church!

While this is *not* a male bashing book, let's face it, ladies. We have all run into these types of men.

After the conversation with my friend, I prayed about what a vacation from men, a Man-kation, really meant for me, and asked God to help me explore the answers. During my journaling, He showed me that it was *"vacation time"* for self-assessment, restoration, and revelation. He showed me that this time would require separation from dating, flirting, and having sex. These things I understood as distractions that would keep me from God's guidance and leave me trapped in the *"wilderness"* of the single life.

God further revealed to me that there is a godly way of *"living single"* that is full of hope, peace, joy and love! I accepted the challenge and prepared myself for the man-kation that was just ahead.

I began by asking these questions. You may want to ask them too:

- Where is the man God has for me?
- Is there something wrong with me?
- Do I *"really"* know what I want in a man?

❖ Why do I keep attracting the same type of man?

These questions cause us to worry even though Jesus says do not worry about anything…

But seek ye first the kingdom of God, and his righteousness; and all these things shall be added unto you.
Matthew 6:33

Together, we're going to explore how God's kingdom takes us from the worries of the *wilderness* to fulfillment in His *Garden (the promised land)* of peace.

God's Garden is our resting place. There we will find serenity and the answers, vision, purpose, and plan that He has for our life! The Promised Land is where we live in the overflow of life. Like the scripture above promises, if we seek God (going through the process) first, *then* what we desire will be given to us.

Let's ponder this: If we have desired to have a husband, why has God not given us one? Let me tell you why--because we are *not* ready!

Because we think we are ready, we start dating, falling for men of "worldly character" and carrying along with us past hurts, regrets, demands and bad attitudes. Then we get frustrated when it doesn't work out and say, "I'm just going to sit back and wait for God." This process happens repeatedly until we realize that we have a part in the whole process too. It is here that God halts us, and something such as a man-kation begins to invade our thoughts.

A man-kation involves us doing our part to get ready for the unique man that God has prepared just for us. Just as a runner prepares for a marathon or a law student prepares to take the bar exam, we *must* prepare for our husbands. God loves His daughters and sons, but both have to be spiritually and emotionally ready for the lifetime commitment of marriage. He is not going to bring His strong son to a weak, un-submissive daughter. Likewise, He is not going to bring His daughter to a weak undisciplined son. Instead, learning to be fully submissive to God will equip us to submit to our own husbands.

Let's see what the Word says about submission:

Wives, be subject (be submissive and adapt yourselves) to your own husbands as [a service] to the Lord. ^{23}For the husband is head of the wife as Christ is the Head of the church, Himself the Savior of [His] body. ^{24}As the church is subject to Christ, so let wives also be subject in everything to their husbands.
Ephesians 5:22-25

How did you feel when you read that scripture? Did you cringe at the thought of being subject to your husband in *everything*? I know I did. To be subject to him with how I spend *my* money, *my* time and how I dress was a hard concept for me to accept before I took a man-kation.

God explained to me that I cringed because of selfishness and spiritual immaturity. He plainly said that was the reason I could not submit to a man or to

Him. Submission to God in every aspect of our lives is a tremendous transformation from darkness into light!

Taking a man-kation is preparation time to get rid of the terrible attitudes, pain from the past, and anything that would hold us back from receiving the promises of God. If we truly want to have a special man in our life, then it's worth the time to get ready for him.

As we get ready, it's necessary to be truthful with ourselves and recognize that we *must* take this time. Not only for a man, but essentially for ourselves, because the most important human relationship we have is with ourselves!

This involves learning to love, being confident and enjoying ourselves. So, when God does send that special person, we can love, be confident and enjoy him! During this time, we gain wisdom on relating to others and we also get answers and begin to understand them.

As we read through this book, by God's grace we will develop wisdom with the right self-discipline and motivations to not only *want* a husband but to be a virtuous wife!

This man-kation will prove to be a time of total transformation. Just as people take vacations to rejuvenate or to simply enjoy themselves; think of our man-kation as if we are going to some remote island to do both because essentially, we are!

Chapter 2
The "Wilderness Man" Search

Man~kation Tip 1: "Focus on God!"

During this man-kation, God wants us all to Himself to show us some things, share some things, and reshape us from the inside out.

One of the first things He showed me was that looking for a man with my old mindset was a *"wilderness search"* that leads to a dead end. I learned—and you will too—how to leave your *wilderness mindset* and enter your new g*arden mindset.*

The word *wilderness* derives from the notion of "wildness." *Wildness* means to be undisciplined, acting on emotions and living with no sense of direction. The wilderness search is like trying to find a needle in a haystack, only the needle doesn't exist. Women are searching for a man when God ordained just the opposite—for a man to find a woman (Proverbs 18:22).

In this regard, the enemy wants us to run around like a "wild horse"—going from man to man—while lying to ourselves and saying, "Next time I'm not going to do this or that," but when the time comes, we end up doing the same thing. We even call ourselves "taking a break from men", but we really don't do a self-assessment and allow God to help us. The enemy knows what our flesh likes, so he sends the *counterfeit man,* and we go right back to the same wilderness.

When we're in the wilderness, we complain to God when things don't work out like we want them to. We even try to blame Him. Then a man comes along, looking, sounding, and acting so good that we are taken aback. Immediately, we're willing to do whatever it takes to get him. But he's counterfeit; once he gets what he wants, his true colors show.

The counterfeit man is everywhere—at work, the gym, the store, and even at church! The devil wants our joy and peace, so he uses the confusion of a counterfeit to keep us in the wilderness. He paints a pretty picture on the outside, but the inside is full of deceit. It's a never ending round and round cycle full of anguish.

Focusing on God is the **only** way to get off the wilderness merry-go-round. Isaiah 54:5 says, "For your maker is your husband." We must focus on our relationship with our "Spiritual Husband" *first* and then the "Physical Husband" *will* manifest!

In the book of Exodus, God chose Moses to lead the Israelites from Egypt through the wilderness to the promised land. The journey should have taken eleven days, but it took forty years! They kept running around the same mountain as lost and confused children.

During this time, God performed many miracles. He fed them food from heaven and delivered them out of slavery. Yet they still had the slave mentality; they doubted God, complained, created other *gods*, and were lovers of their own desires.

This is parallel to our *wilderness search*. The search for a man becomes a god when we focus on finding him. We try online dating, blind dating and acquaintance dating. I'm not saying this type of dating doesn't work, but without God leading and restoring us it will *never* work.

We doubt God by trying to do His job in creating our own blessings and not understanding the process. God knows when we are ready, and He will bring it to pass once we have taken the time to let Him completely heal us!

Wilderness dating can lead to having intimate relationships with men we have no business being with, like married men, broken men "in the church", thieves, abusers, and even bisexual men.

Concerning this *"wilderness search"* Jesus says:

You are of your father, the devil, and it is your will to practice the lusts and gratify the desires [which are characteristic] of your father. He was a murderer from the beginning and does not stand in the truth, because there is no truth in him. When he speaks a falsehood, he speaks what is natural to him, for he is a liar [himself] and the father of lies and of all that is false.

John 8:44

If we are displaying the characteristics of the devil, Jesus calls him our father! When I read this, it blew my mind to think that every time I practiced lust and gratified my desires, I could be considered a child of the devil! This behavior completely separates us from God and keeps us in slavery to the enemy. Even though we know Jesus died for our sins so we can live a life of abundance, our slave-mentality will not allow us to receive it and rest in God's garden.

Some of the lies the devil tells single women is, "All the good men are taken," or "There are no good men (all men are dogs)." Scripture says he is a liar and there is no truth in him. So, when we are in this wilderness, we become slaves to lies. Then out of desperation or fear of being alone, we settle for less, which leads to regret. Depression sets in, and eventually we become tired of being sick and tired.

During my wilderness search, which was really the first time in my adult life that I was single, it only lasted a little over a year, then I became so fed up with the chaos that I had to come out!

I was in my late thirties and completely oblivious to the wild, wild, *wilderness* of dating, but the devil was on the move, roaming, seeking to devour me; constantly taking every opportunity to deceive me. I kept wandering around feeling so confused by the "dating games".

Every time I dated someone, my spirit *never* had peace, and I kept hearing God say, "I have *someone* so much better for you!" I would get my hopes up about someone and then they would get shot down as quickly as they went up—up and down like a roller coaster. I knew I needed a change in my life.

God helped me to realize that dating was a *temporary* bandage for the void that was missing in my life. God *first* is what was missing. My man-kation showed me that the more I focused on God, the less I focused on "finding a man." God completely changed my desires and outlook on life.

He spoke to me every day, and I started to become complete in my spirit. He reminded me of His love through His Word and that He has so many awesome things planned for me! He fulfilled everything I needed, and He kept me in His perfect peace!

> *"When we lose our focus on God, it draws us back to the Wilderness!"*

There will be times while you are on man-kation that you will be tempted to go back to your old mindset or what is familiar. God showed me that I was only tempted by what my flesh wanted. Recognize that your flesh is a slave to sin, but the Word says God gives you power over anything through Him (Philippians 4:13).

I started to pray daily for deliverance from those thoughts and confessed out of my mouth that I would not go back!

Like me, you must *speak* the word of God to those thoughts. Confess out of your mouth that it is done by faith. Remember you are in *total* control of what you think, say, and do! I even asked God so many times to change my thoughts. I wanted to be more like Him and stay in peace. I stayed humble at the feet of Jesus in prayer: "God, I need you. I can't do this without you. I got to have you." He will answer your call and He *will* come to your rescue!

God is so gracious that He has given us some help. The Holy Spirit (our comforter) and grace (God's unmerited favor) will help us to decide *by faith* to come out of the wilderness.

Lean on, trust in, and be confident in the Lord with all your heart and mind and do not rely on your own insight or understanding.
Proverbs 3:5

It is imperative that we *stay out* of the wilderness! A man-kation helps us to lean on God for understanding. He will help us to comprehend why we had the wilderness experiences and why we must seek Him concerning our future. He wrote the story of our lives, so it only makes sense to consult with the Author for direction.

Man~kation Tip 2: "Think like God and you will act like God!"

It's very important to separate ourselves from all the distractions in our lives to spend quality time with God. In these moments, God gives wisdom to take the right route in our lives, and He changes our desires to what *HE* wants for us. And the more we seek Him and inquire of Him, the more we will find Him (Deuteronomy 4:29).

It's called preparation, and it's crucial. Just like any other relationship we have, the more time we spend with anyone the more we become like them. God is no different. He meets us right where we are, and He will guide and comfort us.

There are many examples in the bible where God separated people so He could reveal Himself to them. When Moses received the Ten Commandments, he went up into the mountain by himself. Even Jesus went off by Himself plenty of times to pray and spend time with God. So this is a *must*! Ladies, make time, create time, and spend time with GOD!

Eventually your thoughts will change to resemble His thoughts, and His Word will be written across the tablet of your heart (2 Corinthians 3:3). The Holy Spirit abides in you, so He will constantly direct you in the way to go. This will create a strong spirit within you that will cause your flesh/emotions to become weak to God's will.

These are the required beginning steps to coming out of the wilderness. This time is the "rest" we need to break away from the wilderness lies and deceptions; to gain strength and hear from God concerning our lives.

We must *always* recognize God in everything that we do to see if it imitates Him, and if not, *keep it moving*! We must fight every day to beat off that old man by renewing our mind. Say to yourself, "I am not a slave to sin!" It is extremely serious that we come out of the wilderness quickly. I did, and I am confident that you will too!

Man~kation Tip 3:
"Repentance equals total restoration!"

For godly grief and the pain God is permitted to direct, produce a repentance that leads and contributes to salvation and deliverance from evil, and it never brings regret; but worldly grief (the hopeless sorrow that is characteristic of the pagan world) is deadly [breeding and ending in death].
2 Corinthians 7:10

The Word reminds us that we will *never* regret repentance. No condemnation (Romans 8:1)! Jesus paid the price for sin. By asking for forgiveness with a sincere and grieved heart brings it to pass. God knows what to permit in our lives to get us to the point of repentance. The wilderness is full of hopelessness and shame, but repentance is full of freedom and happiness!

When I went on my man-kation, the reality of my backslidden state and not putting God first became heavy on my heart. I knew that God did not approve, and it brought *Him* sorrow (Ephesians 4:30).

The closer I got to Him, the more I grieved *with* Him and repented from a genuine heart. This was the starting point for my process of total restoration!

We cannot enter into His peace, joy, and love …His Garden, *without* repentance! I thank God for His forgiveness of my sins. Romans 3:22 says; "We are righteous by faith in Jesus." All we have to do is *believe* that Jesus was crucified for our sins and then we are made righteous. The law of sin brings death, but it is the blood of Jesus that gives us God's grace to overcome sin (Romans 8:2).

For God so loved the world that he gave his only begotten Son, that whosoever believeth in him should not perish, but have everlasting life.
$\qquad\qquad\qquad\qquad\qquad\qquad\qquad$ John 3:16

Once you confess your sins and confess Jesus as your Savior, then you are saved and will have eternal life with God!

Pray this prayer:

Lord, I ask in the name of Jesus for you to forgive me for all my sins, known and unknown to me. I know that I chose to commit them and ask that you give me strength to overcome the temptations in my life. I confess Jesus Christ as my Lord and Savior. God, I want you to be the center of my life. I ask you to open my heart to your spirit, so that my mind is renewed in you! Lord, as I read this book, I pray that I receive revelation for *my life*!

In Jesus name AMEN!

If you just said that prayer, you are on your way to your NEW life in Christ!

Chapter 3

How a Man-kation can heal your broken heart

The first time my heart was broken was when my father died. I was seventeen years old, and my father was the first man whom I truly loved. God woke me up one morning while I was on my man-kation and revealed this to me. I always thought it was my first boyfriend, but my father's death was the first real scar in my heart.

I was a "daddy's girl". I looked just like him and he adored me. I remember sitting on his lap watching the Lakers game or standing on his feet dancing with him.

My father was 6'3, dark skinned, nice curly hair with a big, beautiful smile. He was very intelligent, articulate, and athletic. To say that we were close is an understatement. Even though my parents separated when I was about nine years old, I still saw him often. I was his shadow and enjoyed my time with him to the fullest.

I recall the night my father died. I was out with some friends at a party. Suddenly, I had this feeling that something was terribly wrong. I told my friends that I wanted to go home. When I arrived home, everyone was ok, but then about four o'clock in the morning the phone rang. I sat straight up in my bed knowing something was wrong. My mother answered my aunt's call, telling her that my father had died. I heard my mom scream and ran downstairs and grabbed the phone. My aunt said, "Baby, your daddy is gone, he died last night." I screamed, "No! Why"? Then I dropped the phone, fell on the floor, and laid there crying for hours.

My father was thirty-nine years old and died from a brain aneurysm. It was one of the most devastating events in my life.

Soon after his death I became rebellious, blaming my mother because if my parents were together, she could have taken him to the doctor sooner, mad at my father because he left me and I thought he should have taken better care of himself, and I was upset at God because I felt like I didn't have enough time with my father. His life was cut short, and I didn't understand why.

During my man-kation, God showed me that time heals all wounds and my father's death was not for me to judge, place blame on, or use as an excuse to walk around hurt. I had to understand that it was God's will, and there was nothing I could have done to stop my father's death. I also came to the realization that I was using my father's death as an excuse for my shortcomings, which kept me from taking responsibility for my mistakes. I had to let go of the hurt and learn to trust God in everything, and that was just the first time.

The second time my heart was broken was a couple of years later. After my father's death, I was very vulnerable, still aching due to the loss. That's when I met my first real boyfriend whom I was so deeply in love with. He was more mature than guys I went to high school with and had traveled the world. He was 4 years older than me, and just like my father he was an ex-Navy man (setup number 1).

The enemy was setting me up to kill and destroy me. During my man-kation God showed me that, *I kept looking for my father's love in the men I chose to be with.* When a man had anything in common with my dad, I immediately (subconsciously) became attached to him. Many women have this issue—If their fathers are missing in their lives (for whatever reason), they become very vulnerable because of that emptiness.

After I graduated from high school, I received a lump sum of money from my father's death. I used it to buy a brand-new car and my boyfriend influenced me to get an apartment with him (set up number 2). Once we got into our own apartment, he would stay out late, have female phone numbers in his pockets and even wrecked my new car. I thought that he was the only man that would ever love me.

He didn't physically hurt me but mentally he was tearing down my self-esteem.

The constant cheating and lying made me feel like I wasn't good enough for him. I felt rejected and completely heartbroken after our breakup. That was when I promised myself that I would *never* let a man hurt me like that again. The setup of being rejected and untrusting of men made me build walls with *all* men that lasted for years!

Rejection is something that we have all experienced at some point in our lives. It tears down your self-esteem and makes you unsure of yourself, which makes you not trust anyone, including yourself. *Wisdom* says if that person was for you, then they would *still* be with you, and they would have loved you the way God wants you to be loved.

Man~kation Tip 4:
"Rejection is God's protection!"

God protects you from the plot of the enemy, so the rejection is His way of protecting *His* plans for you. I quickly learned through my reflection time with

God that He was protecting me for *His* ultimate purpose. I had to be rejected because those people had no *future* purpose in my life.

The man God has for you will NEVER reject you, but he will protect you! He will protect your heart, your reputation, your goals, your weakness, and your strengths!

There is a rejection from other people that can cause heartbreak as well. An example would be a friend or family member that betrays you. This type of heartbreak sometimes comes from offense, which causes us to have pity parties that, if prolonged, can lead to depression and even suicide. The devil has a plan to kill and destroy you, but Jesus came to restore you! This man-kation that you are taking is your refuge from the continual schemes of the enemy.

But thou, O LORD, art a shield for me; my glory, and the lifter up of mine head.
                                        Psalm 3:3
Jesus is the lifter up of your head. Rejection causes a lot of humiliation, which makes you feel less than the person God has ordained you to be.

Jesus said, "Call on my name and I will lift up your head with my love." He was rejected by a multitude in so many ways and is still rejected to this day. His disciple Peter denied Him three times, and Judas betrayed Him. Imagine the agony He had to endure knowing that these two men He loved and walked with would turn their backs on Him. Jesus has firsthand experience with rejection, and He fully understands our hurts and disappointments.

Man~kation Tip 5:
"Unforgiveness keeps you broken."

In my early twenties, I married a man who was emotionally disconnected. He and I both had so much hurt. He was in the military and was the first guy I seriously dated after the big break up. He was a good financial provider, which I thought was all I needed in my life. We had children, houses, cars, and took regular family vacations, but I was still unhappy. I would walk around with a mask— a smile on my face— but on the inside I was despondent and displeased.

I always felt like there should be more to life. I repressed the pain so much that I started to accept it as a part of my life. I would often wonder what happened to that little girl that had so much hope for the future. I couldn't understand why I just could not be happy. We tried marriage counseling several times, but needless to say, after thirteen years our marriage was over.

To add to my misery, my ex-husband remarried just *three weeks* after our divorce. This caused me to immediately get into a relationship (out of retaliation) with a man that completely deceived me by taking me all the way to the altar but was still married to another woman!

Those experiences added more (heartbreak) unforgiveness, distrust, and unbelief that a man could love me the way I desired to be loved. But God had shown me how a man should treat me with my father's love, so I couldn't understand why those men could not fill that void. The memory of those situations kept bringing back the hurt and anger, which was destroying my life.

Forgiveness is something that we all must do to be set free from our broken hearts.

During my man-kation, I cried out to God and asked Him to heal my broken heart. Suddenly, I began to realize that God's love was the only thing I needed to heal my heart (fill the void). God's wisdom helped me to recognize that as long as I allowed the past hurt to affect my future then that person had power over my life.

Now having received the Holy Spirit, and being [a]led and directed by Him] if you forgive the sins of anyone, they are forgiven; if you retain the sins of anyone, they are retained.
                                              John 20:23

This scripture clearly shows us that we must *not* hold on to any hurt against any man or anyone for anything! If we do, then eventually it will come out in a new relationship, so we must deal with this issue. Now let's reflect on our past relationships to see if there is any unforgiveness.

Ladies, take a moment and think about the man that broke your heart.

- ❖ If you saw him today, what would you say to him?
- ❖ How would you feel if you saw him with another woman?

Realize that Hurt is an emotion of Unforgiveness!

Be *truthful* with yourself.

- ❖ Would you *really* be able to speak to him with *love*?
- ❖ Could you truly hope that he is living a good life?

I don't care if he is a baby-daddy that *never* paid child support or an ex-husband who cheated or beat you. We must only have love and loving thoughts towards him. If not, there is still unforgiveness in your heart.

While forgiveness is one of the keys to freedom and healing, *forgiveness does not happen overnight*;

there is a process of understanding, and by using wisdom it will get you there.

I want you to *acknowledge* that there is some hurt and unforgiveness toward these men so you can *start* the healing process. Remember God's grace will give you the strength to overcome the hurt and disappointment. His grace gives you wisdom to understand the *lessons learned* and to *let go* so you can move forward in your life.

Gaining Wisdom

Man~kation Tip 6:
"Forgive Everyone for Everything!"

How can we say, "I'm ready for a husband" and still hold on to hurt from the past?

How can we expect to have a good relationship with a man, or anyone, and walk around broken-hearted? How can we really enjoy our life and be full of regret?

Let's look at unforgiveness from God's perspective.

For if you forgive other people when they sin against you, your heavenly Father will also forgive you. [15] *but if you do not forgive others their sins, your Father will not forgive your sins.*

                                        Matthew 6:14-15

I always thought that all I needed to do was ask God in Jesus's name for forgiveness, and I was forgiven. I was not *really* focusing on forgiving others. Then God showed me that *if* I don't forgive those who have wronged me, then I will *not* be able to receive His forgiveness.

You being able to receive forgiveness from God is connected to your forgiving others!

God does forgive us, but to truly be able to receive *His* forgiveness we must be able to forgive. If not, condemnation will keep us bound to bitterness and doubt. If we can't understand how to forgive someone, then we really won't be able to comprehend how God can forgive us!

This was such a life-changing lesson about forgiveness for me. It truly helped me to walk in God's forgiveness! Now I know that when I ask

God to forgive me, I can go away with a free heart knowing I am forgiven. Once you forgive by letting the hurt go and *choosing* to love, you start to live with freedom from offense, resentment, and the bondage of hurt (*heart healed*)!

God has a plan for our lives, and we must recognize that our wilderness experiences had to happen to get us to the place where we are today. Dealing with the pain we experienced is all a part of the process in making us strong. When we walk about easily offended, unforgiveness and hurt can distract us from God's plan.

When you are ill-treated by someone, think about the cross. Jesus said, "Forgive them Father, for they know not what they do" (Luke 23-34). Jesus prayed that God would forgive those that were guilty of torturing Him, even unto death. He took no account for His hurt. Now that is forgiveness to the *definitive level,* when you can lovingly pray for those that mistreat you!

Proverbs 24:7 says, "Wisdom is too high for a fool." Remember that 24/7!

This proverb will keep you from being easily offended or involved in foolish disagreements. You can promptly identify that some people just lack the wisdom to understand or to be rational. Holding on to this proverb will also make you think like Jesus— "they *really* don't know what they are doing." This will help you to not look down on others but to have compassion for them.

Furthermore, we must use this example of godly wisdom to understand it's *not* the person who hurt us, it is an evil spirit using the person to sidetrack us. When we can separate the person from the evil spirit, that's power, and walking in forgiveness & love becomes easier!

God also reminded me during my man-kation of the people I had hurt. We all have hurt someone, no one is exempt. I realized that I could have handled it better, and if given another chance I probably would.

God gave me mercy, forgiveness, and showed me love in those situations. Now I think the same way about those that hurt me. I must give them *mercy & forgiveness* even if I "feel" like they intentionally hurt me and have no remorse for it.

God reveals the root of your issues in the heartbreak area of your life. He showed me that this type of hurt is *very deep* and said this concerning man that have broken our hearts:

> "**Understand the part YOU played in your brokenheartedness and move on!**"

Man~kation Tip 7: "Never forget the lessons learned!"

As I matured in Him, I realized that my past was not about the mistakes I made, but it was about the lessons I learned. I focused on the fact that God was always my instructor, and the lessons are required to protect me from repeating my mistakes. Once I learned the lesson, then I could completely understand the how and why.

Before I had this perspective, I continuously got upset about the mistakes that I made. The lessons I learned and continue to learn through wisdom are invaluable!

The first thing about learning lessons is to identify that there were warning signs, but our selfishness in wanting that man blinded us to the reality of who that man really was. The saying is true that "People only do to you what you allow them to." You knew the man was a liar and a cheat, but you stayed. You knew that he was an abuser from the first time he hit you, but you didn't leave. You knew he was a bum (not wanting to work), but you stayed and had kids with him!

I'm not saying these things to place all the blame on us. However, there were some things we knew, but we kept going forward in these bad relationships and ended up heartbroken. Sometimes women like to dismiss things by blaming men, but that is *not* the way to get healed!

I have learned to appreciate the *lessons* learned from every *wrong* man! They have helped me *immediately* identify when one of their "teammates" shows up. I no longer am fooled by their slick words or their good looks. I am only impressed by a man's spirit.

God has given us *his* discernment to know the difference between a *counterfeit man* and *a real man*, but it's our choice to be a *fool* (emotional) or to be *focused* (wise)!

Man~kation Tip 8:
"Deal with the hurt; it's the only way to be healed!"

God created us as these wonderful, understanding, and trusting human beings. He gave us the physical ability to carry life inside of us and then give birth to that life as natural caregivers.

We care for others (our children, family, and friends) but we can sometimes forget about ourselves and don't want to face the reality of our lives. So, we sweep our issues under the rug because we don't want to deal with the pain, which causes us to jump from one relationship to another or to shut down and live a lonely life.

Not dealing with hurt will have you on an emotional rollercoaster, which can cause you to keep making the same mistakes repeatedly. We can carry grudges, hurt, offense, regret, and disappointment inside us; which gives birth to all sorts of negative emotions; selfishness, ego, insecurity, fear, judgment, envy, jealousy, and so on.

It's time to *stop* living on emotions, *stop* sweeping things under the rug and time to *stop* blaming others!

It's time to take care of ourselves and pull the rug back. No one else can do this for us. It is our responsibility to tackle these issues. No matter how much it hurts or how much we want to forget about them, we must ask and rely on God to give us the strength to reflect on the part we played.

As a mature Christian, you must be able to control your emotions to display the character of Christ. Look at yourself and don't make any excuses or blame someone else. Remember the part that you played in your broken heartedness and move on. I can certainly recall many instances where I had warning signs but did not yield or stop.

The hurt that we carry prevents us from moving into a positive direction in our lives. Women pass the hurt they received from one man to the next. The only way to really love a man is to be totally healed from a broken heart so you can love him with a pure heart. If you're not ready to deal with these issues in the deep part of the ocean (your heart), then you will stay in the wilderness.

You may die out there and only get a glimpse of the promised land through the other women around you!

Man~kation Tip 9:
"Forgive yourself; Forget regret!"

Did you know that you can break your own heart?

Now that we are taking responsibility for our part in being brokenhearted, it's very important that we forgive ourselves to keep our inner peace and self-love. There were so many times I wanted to kick myself for doing something that was foolish. I have to admit, there were also times when I didn't like myself because I had so much regret.

When we make wrong decisions, it builds up regret that we can carry for years. This regret will lead to self-hatred, which breaks your heart, and then you start to doubt and not trust yourself. This is another one of our deepest hurts— because if you don't trust yourself, then how can you trust anyone else?

When you forgive yourself, you start to trust yourself and your decisions. This trust helps you to begin to love yourself and take responsibility for your actions. You cannot make any wise changes or decisions until you are ready to accept responsibility. When you mature to take responsibility for your actions, you do something about them—you make better decisions!

He heals the brokenhearted and binds up their wounds [curing their pains and their sorrows].
                                          Psalm 147:3

Jesus will mend your heart back together with His love—one hurt at a time. Healing comes from letting go of all the questions around the situation and just forgiving. I cried about my hurt, then I listened to God's voice say, "My child, count it all joy, for I have something great planned for you!" That was my moment of hope and then He gave me a vision of my future!

Once I got a revelation of His love for me, it started to heal my broken heart. I realized that I took God's love for granted, and yet He still provided and loved me. I also understood and believed that I could be loved by someone special and that I deserved the best!

This helped me with restoring my confidence and also gave me the courage to take down the walls I had built up. I know that God loved me even when I rejected Him! I now have so much compassion for the broken hearted and want them to be healed completely— like I did with God's love!

And hope does not disappoint us, because God has poured out his love into our hearts by the Holy Spirit, whom he has given us.
Romans 5:5

Seal your heart with God's love, knowing that He has poured out Himself in you! I want you to meditate on God's love for you *daily*. Get it embedded in your mind that God loves you no matter what you've done or what the situation is.

Say to yourself, *"God loves me!"* Get it ingrained in your heart that He cares for you. He thinks of you at all times, He adores you, and He wants to please you! That keeps you full of hope and keeps you completely healed from the broken heart you once had.

Chapter 4
Avoid the Tricks
of the Enemy

When it comes to our man-kation God showed me that many of us have a problem with temptation. The sad part is the enemy knows exactly what buttons to push. So, during this chapter we'll talk about those buttons and how to transform your mind to *remove* them!

Man~kation Tip 10:
"Living a life in the flesh is a mess!"

When I was in the wilderness, I often confused *lust* with *love.* Because wilderness dating is full of confusion, we're constantly being deceived by the enemy's tricks—everything is dramatic! The flesh needs to be fulfilled in its desires to feel satisfied, which causes lustful dating. Let's begin with identifying some things that are done during lustful dating, so we can stop being manipulated by enemy's tactics.

Characteristics of lustful dating

1. **Lies** – If a man lies to you or you lie to him just to stay involved with one another.

2. **Confusion** – If you are confused about him, but you still try to stay connected to him.

3. **Desiring a man by simply looking at him** – Love at first sight.

4. **Impatient** – Rushing to be together. Love is Patient!

5. **Wrong Intentions** – If you want him for his money or as a trophy (status or looks)!

6. **Sexual Lust** – Having nothing in common but sex!

Lies

Why is it that when we meet a man (in the wilderness), we tell lies? We lie about our age, the number of children we have, our education level, and even our careers.

The wilderness is all about competition with other women, so we try to make ourselves more appealing to get a man. It is a trick of the enemy. Eventually you find out that the man is lying as well. The competition to impress one another is very deceiving, and the relationship is doomed to fail.

Confusion

The enemy creates a fantasy about a man for you based on lies. Once things don't add up you become confused, and because your flesh is brought into the lies, you can't let him go. The flesh continues to live in the fantasy of who this man is *supposed* to be, and, in the end, you feel very foolish!

Desiring a Man by simply looking at Him

To desire a man by looking at him is completely operating in the flesh! It's ok to see a nice-looking man and think he is attractive, but to see him and think you've got to have him or that you're in love, is ridiculous.

Many women become fixated with men based on how they look; and if they have sex with these men it's over— the enemy has them! Their fantasy turns into obsession about having a "real" relationship with these men. The men lie and manipulate so much that eventually the women become entangled in a "sex-buddy" relationship and have no idea how they got there.

Impatience

Impatience happens when people don't want to take the time for love to develop, so they rush into a relationship for various reasons. I found that in the church, a couple will rush into marriage so they can have sex or validate their reason for already having sex. This is extremely dangerous, because marriage as we know, is a lifetime commitment; and when you marry someone you really don't know, it is another trick of the enemy and a set up for divorce!

Wrong Intentions

Most women in the wilderness are aggressive and superficial; they enjoy trying to impress their friends and family with a man based on his financial status or his looks. The lust of material things, money, and how people see them validates them; it pleases the flesh with vanity. Most of the time they have nothing in common with these men and the man is also using the women for their own intent. The enemy's trick is that the people they are trying to impress know it, so they are really only fooling themselves!

Sexual Lust

I saved this one for last because I believe this is the riskiest characteristic of them all. When a person is completely driven by sex, they do all sorts of immoral things. The selfishness of only wanting to please the flesh with sex becomes a drug for them, so they become greedy in wanting it all the time with anyone. They don't care about whom they hurt or even hurting themselves. This type of behavior involves being careless, including having unprotected sex with multiple partners. The trick of the enemy is to make you feel good temporarily but to destroy you permanently physically. We must be pleased with ourselves and honor ourselves *permanently* instead of the *temporary* pleasure of sex.

Many Christians don't like to discuss this subject, but we cannot avoid it because it is a huge problem in the church. Many people go to church every Sunday; and when they leave church, go back to their "secret sin" of having sex with people that are *not* their spouses. We don't have to admit to each other, but God knows the truth, and he is *not* pleased.

A Man-kation will give you victory over lustful behavior!

That each one of you should know how to possess (control, manage) his own body in consecration (purity, separated from things profane) and honor,5Not [to be used] in the passion of lust like the heathen, who are ignorant of the true God and have no knowledge of His will.
1 Thessalonians 4:4-5

We must learn and grow in the things of God—keep pressing, keep holding on to Him, keep praying! You have to make time for God, or you will *never* be able to have control over yourself. Every right decision you make changes every bad decision you made. Meaning, every time you submit yourself (doing things God's way), you are in God's will, which plants good seeds for your life.

We are not ignorant to God's will, His purpose, and His precepts. He has laid everything out for us in the Word. We must honor the Word to produce His will in our life! He wants us to submit ourselves unto Him by dying to our old lustful ways of acting like we have no knowledge of who we are *in* Him.

He wants us to separate ourselves from perverse things and consecrate ourselves to regain our purity.

So be subject to God. Resist the devil [stand firm against him], and he will flee from you.
James 4:7

Resistance means to withstand or stand firm against! When we resist the enemy, he will come back with his buddies, so we must be strong in not running from him but to stand against him! Not fearing him because people only run from things they are intimidated by. You must know that "Greater is He that *lives* in you, than he in the world" (1 John 4:4)! You have the spirit of the highest, most Powerful God living inside you. There is *never* any reason to be afraid of the enemy—he is already defeated and *cannot* do anything to harm you!

With that being said, the only way to really resist the enemy is to allow God to remove the lustful temptations in your life by the renewing of your mind. Temptations are how the enemy draws us back into the wilderness. He is the master of deception; he presents a question or a situation to tempt you. It's the only weapon he has; he knows what lusts are in us because he put them there.

When you can distinguish the difference between *lust* and *love*, you become strong against the tricks of the enemy. We must change the way we think about meeting a man, dating a man, and being in a relationship with a man!

And be not conformed to this world: but be ye transformed by the renewing of your mind, that ye may prove what is that good, and acceptable, and perfect, will of God.
Romans 12:2

The transformation in your mind is the essential element in taking complete authority over lustful thinking, lustful speaking, and lustful actions. Only by God's grace does He impart His power to fully change our way of thinking. We must be willing to submit/present ourselves (sacrifice our old ways) to God for this transformation to take place.

This transformation of the mind causes your flesh to push buttons. Every time it doesn't get what it wants, it will:

- Throw tantrums: "I want it now!"

- Try to reason with you: "Ok, just one more time!"

- Lie to you: "It's not a sin to fornicate, if we love each other and will be married soon."

- Get mad: "You are so stupid; he was the best man you ever had and you're not getting any younger!"

Man~kation Tip 11:
"Never compromise with the Flesh"

The word says that we must always stay alert and pray that through grace, and we will resist temptation (Matthew 26:41). The enemy is always on the prowl trying to see whom he can devour. The spirit that is in us does not sin; however, the flesh is weak to sin and will continue to draw you back. The more that you resist the flesh, the weaker it will become in that area. But you must *always* be aware that it is there.

Temptations are in our heart; it is a heart condition; we must ask God to change our hearts desires.

Someone once told me that God is good when He wants to be. I immediately told him that God is *always* good. We are the ones that walk away from His goodness, being led by our fleshly desires. Once we go out too far, we look back and try to blame God for our situation.

Say this daily prayer:

Let the words of my mouth and the meditation of my heart be acceptable in Your sight, O Lord, my [firm, impenetrable] Rock and my Redeemer.
Psalm 19:14

To *successfully* abstain from your temptations, you *must* have the right heart condition and understand that they are stronghold thoughts that you have the power to kick out of your thinking!

I had to say out loud, "I have the mind of Christ" so many times when my flesh was acting up. To be a soldier for God, you must be strong, knowing that the weapon of our warfare is not physical but spiritual (2 Corinthians 10:4-5). Walking in the Spirit by meditating on the word and confessing out of your mouth is all you need to win the fight with your flesh!

Yet amid all these things we are more than conquerors and gain a surpassing victory through Him Who loved us.
Romans 8:37

In the spirit we have already conquered the enemy, so now it's time to confess it out of our mouth and stand against his tricks!

To stand firm against temptation you must

- Keep an active prayer life!

- Keep your guard up daily (stay watchful of old thoughts)!

- Stay committed to your boundaries!

- Don't play with the enemy (or try to compromise).

- Don't ignore the voice of God.

- Read the word of God!

Once we change our thoughts, we change our hearts. God's goodness and His power will give us the upper hand to overcome *all* temptations!

Chapter 5
Walk in Wisdom

Strip yourselves of your former nature [put off and discard your old un renewed self] which characterized your previous manner of life and becomes corrupt through lusts and desires that spring from delusion; ^{23}And be constantly renewed in the spirit of your mind [having a fresh mental and spiritual attitude]
Ephesians 4:22-23

During my man-kation, stripping off the "old-me" to put on the "new-me" was like ripping off a Band-Aid repeatedly—it hurt!!

Wisdom helped me to continually stay focused on developing my new mind; however, there was a lot of emotional pain. One of the first pains I felt was loneliness. God separated me from everyone and everything so that I could totally focus on Him. This was to develop an intimacy with Him so that I would know when He was speaking to me.

This separation blocks out *all* disturbances to hear His voice, so His changes can take place in your mind. The only way to really walk in wisdom is to learn the voice of God.

Think about when you're at work and you leave your family and friends to focus on your job. This could not be achieved successfully with distractions. It's the same with God; to get the job done for your renewed mind, you need a getaway.

You must do your part by changing your phone habits, TV habits, Internet habits, and limiting your conversations. Moderation is the key! Keep God in your eyes, ears and mouth; meaning, read the Word, listen to the Word, and speak/sing the Word. These things are the only ways to stay focused on Him and keep the loneliness from taking over. Please know that change brings adversity. Your family and friends will think you have lost your mind!

I had to learn how to weigh everything by walking in wisdom. When your phone rings with male callers or someone you know God would not approve of (a person that wants to gossip or talk negatively), don't answer it! I eventually changed my phone number (a number that I had for about ten years)! Doing so gave me such freedom and power! I had *total* control over who called me and completely cut ties with people that God did not purpose for my future!

It's time to grow up! God wants us to be strong, mature Christians; making these changes helps you to develop godly character. As you obey God, He will automatically give you wisdom to stop the old way of thinking and acting.

Man~kation Tip 12: "Control your Emotions by walking in Wisdom!"

When we control our emotions by walking in wisdom, it keeps us protected from evil (Proverbs 2:10-12). We will have disappointments in the future but *not* devastations!

Understand that emotions are unstable and change like the weather. "Fickle, foolish, feelings" is what I call the negative emotions we possess by which the enemy enters our mind. Once we meditate on them, they build up tremendous hindrances in our lives.

As you read this book, I would advise you to also read a chapter of Proverbs a day. Proverbs is the *wisdom* book of the Bible. There are thirty-one chapters, so if you read a chapter a day by the end of a month you will have a wealth of wisdom, knowledge, and understanding.

"A chapter of Proverbs a day will keep the foolishness away!"

Forsake not [Wisdom], and she will keep, defend, and protect you; love her, and she will guard you. ⁷The beginning of Wisdom is: get Wisdom (skillful and godly Wisdom)! [For skillful and godly Wisdom is the principal thing.] And with all you have gotten, get understanding (discernment, comprehension, and interpretation).
Proverbs 4:6-7

The word says that wisdom is the principal thing!

- Wisdom will keep you from *"putting your foot in your mouth."*
- Wisdom will defend you when your enemies come against you.
- Wisdom will protect you from living on an emotional roller coaster!
- Wisdom is the *most important* thing to guarding your thoughts.
- Wisdom will help you with your future dating!

Wisdom helps you to think before you speak.
Godly wisdom gives you discernment through the Holy Spirit that will give you the words to say and how to say them, or just to remain silent. The word of God says, "Be quick to hear, slow to speak, slow to take offense, and slow to anger" (James 1:19). When we are quick to listen, it helps us to clearly understand what the other person is saying. This gives you time to think about your response. Wisdom, via the Holy Spirit encourages you to *speak life* in any situation. So, remember to choose

your words *wisely* and don't let your words choose you!

Wisdom defends you against your enemies!

Think about when Jesus was questioned by the high priest and Pilate repeatedly about who He was (Matthew 27:11-14). He answered them directly. He did not argue or try to defend Himself and even remained silent at times. His wisdom in knowing that His words and actions were from God kept Him humble and at peace. When people talk about you or try to attack you, let your character of godly wisdom fight your battle. Keep your peace and be confident in knowing the battle is not yours, it's the Lord's (2 Chronicles 20:15)! This will help you to stop being easily offended, which will create an emotionally strong spirit within you!

A. Renee Wilson

Wisdom will protect you from living on an Emotional Roller Coaster!

Dating in the wilderness is an emotional ride full of twists, turns, ups and downs. When you first meet a man and become fond of him, you have so many hopes of a good relationship. As soon as the newness wears off and reality sets in, you realize that you could not have loved him; it was only lust or infatuation. You could not have really wanted him; it was only the emotion of *something new* that had you *temporarily* excited! It's like buying a new car that you can't afford; at first you are so thrilled and want to drive everywhere to show it off. Once the car payments start stacking up, you realize that you purchased it out of emotions.

Wisdom will help you to develop patience in your entire decision-making process. Your actions will be based on facts and not fantasy!

Wisdom helps you discern in all areas of your life, especially in choosing your man!

When you walk in godly wisdom and meet a man, the second thing you are looking for is his godly spirit. I said the second thing because we all know that the first thing will be his outer appearance (just keeping it real, ladies)! However, it will be his *godly spirit*— the way he talks, acts, and his lifestyle— that will attract your spirit to him, and *that* will determine if he's a keeper or not. I'm not saying that he will be perfect, no one is, but you should be able to clearly see God in him! Only walking in wisdom will show how to determine that. I don't care how nice-looking, smart, or how much money he may have, keep your thoughts on his inner man (his spirit). This will keep you from straying away, making excuses or second guessing. You will no longer be fooled by the enemy and his counterfeit man. Listen closely to the Spirit and please separate your emotions—*just trust the facts of what you know in the spirit and not emotions of what you feel!*

A. Renee Wilson

Wisdom helps to build boundaries for your Future Dating!

The decision to stop dating while on man-kation is so you can gain godly wisdom in this area of your life. Building boundaries around your thoughts by harmonizing everything with the word of God is vital to your survival! Always consider what you are thinking about and then balance it with the facts/standards that you live by! The Holy Spirit is always there to help you to determine if you are trying to cross that line. When your emotions or even your environment says *yes*, guard your thoughts and say *no* if need be! Once you gain wisdom in your decision making, it builds assurance to live with no fear when dating. I'm not saying that you will never make a mistake, but what I am saying is that you won't make the *same* mistakes!

We have dated our way and have failed at finding that special one, so now it's time to do it God's way. The Holy Spirit will let you know when you are ready to start dating again and will tell you *who* to date.

Attraction on the surface only pleases those with a foolish heart. Wisdom searches for the most inner parts—that's the *most* attractive part of a person. The parts of the heart and soul are for the *wise heart*! You've got to go deeper for a keeper!!

The boundaries that you set concerning dating are very important. God will give you specifically what they are for you (pray about it). Make sure you write them down in a place that will be easy for you to reference at first, but once you gain complete strength in this area it will come naturally. These boundaries will help you to focus on "purpose dating" and not "social dating"!

He who gains Wisdom loves his own life; he who keeps understanding shall prosper and find good.

Proverbs 19:8

A. Renee Wilson

When we find wisdom, we find our *true* life, the life God desires for us to have. Truly understanding wisdom and cherishing it, will cause you to prosper in all you do! If you love your life and want better things you *must* gain wisdom!

A wise and powerful woman once said,

Watch your thoughts for they become words.
Watch your words for they become actions.
Watch your actions for they become habits.
Watch your habits for they become your character.
And watch your character for it becomes your destiny.
What we think, we become.

~Margaret Thatcher

Chapter 6

Love is a Characteristic not just an Emotion

Love endures long and is patient and kind; love is never envious nor boils over with jealousy, is not boastful or vainglorious, does not display itself haughtily ⁵It is not conceited (arrogant and inflated with pride); it is not rude (unmannerly) and does not act unbecomingly. Love (God's love in us) does not insist on its own rights or its own way, for it is not self-seeking; it is not touchy or fretful or resentful; it takes no account of the evil done to it [it pays no attention to a suffered wrong].
1 Corinthians 13:4-5

Love is *the* characteristic of Jesus. He represents every word in this scripture; He is such a perfect being. He is love and love is He! The understanding of what love is will help you to develop the personality of Christ.

Many people think that love is just an emotion. For example, if you cry over a man that disappointed you then you must have loved him. Not true at all! The enemy plays on our emotions all of the time. God is not like that; He is the spirit of truth. Emotions are indecisive. Your heart (emotions) will tell you that you are in love, but your mind (your spirit) will totally disagree because there will be no contentment about him. This is a firm indication that love is far more than just a heart condition (emotions).

Your mind is where your thoughts are, and your heart is the seat of your emotions. Your thoughts are the "motherboard" of your life; meaning, wherever your thoughts lead you, you shall go. As we have already talked about, when we become connected to God, our thoughts will be like His thoughts. Always remember the characteristics of love to determine the standards you live by. These standards will create a loving, patient, and kind spirit within you.

Walking in love is spiritual warfare at its best!

Not just with a man but with everyone, Jesus said the greatest commandment is to love your God and to love your neighbor (Matthew 22:37-39). Enduring love is developed by being committed and long-suffering, to love someone without paying attention to your negative emotions.

When we develop this godly endurance, it builds our faith, our testimony, and helps us to walk in *godly love* with everyone in every situation! The endurance of love is a godly characteristic that compels us to stay the same in good times and bad.

Godly endurance says, "God, I'm going to trust you even when I don't see the change in my life yet!" ***Godly endurance*** says, "I'm going to treat people with love even though they disrespect me!"

Jesus learned obedience through what He suffered!
Hebrews 5:8

Your "love walk" is an active portrayal of your obedience to God. Jesus is our example of how to walk in love with your enemies, difficult people, ex-boyfriends, and everyone. Developing this love walk is the foundation of your relationship with your future mate! Show obedience in your character (actions) *not* your emotions. As you can see there is a *huge* difference!

You have to be willing to die to your emotions and rise above them. This dying causes you to suffer in your flesh because it's used to getting its way, proving its point, and having the last word. Once you *decide* to starve your flesh, your spirit will take over and help you to obey God.

This reminds me of the Commissioned song, "Love isn't love until you give it away." There will be situations in relationships when we will not get our way. There will be times when we will not understand our husband, friends, and family (people)! But we must push through our selfishness of wanting our way and just choose to walk in love with our words and actions.

In comparison to men, we must recognize that *men are wired differently than us!* That's the way God described it to me. He said, "I created them one way and created you another." Acknowledging that there are some things we will just *never* understand about men helps us in our love walk with them. We must continue to keep this in our thoughts when we are involved in a relationship with them.

Please understand that...

We don't have to always have the last word!

We don't have to ask, "what about me?"

We don't have to be jealous about his sports, friends, or other women!

We don't have to complain about everything!

We do have to be patient with him.

We do have to accept who he is and not try to change him.

We do need to be kind to him and respect his decisions.

We do have to be confident and secure in our relationship with him.

These things take time to develop, but with a heart that really wants to satisfy God (being submissive) it can be accomplished. Every characteristic of love can only be achieved by recognizing *your* responsibility to take control of *your* emotions/ego, which dictates your actions. We will talk about "killing your ego" later in this book.

Ladies, we should focus on our character (who we are on the inside)— our integrity, how we treat people, and our purpose to attract *real* love!

Your beauty will get you "puppy" love, your heart will get you "fantasy" love, but your character will get you "real" love!

Man~kation Tip 13: "Walk in love - Attract love!"

Love comes when you like yourself, are confident in yourself and trust yourself! When it shows up you won't hesitate to reveal yourself! That kind of *love* is liberty, purity and *forever*. You ought to love and be happy with yourself to share that with someone else. After all, how can you give something that you do not have?

Love yourself on the inside and let your light shine on the outside. As women of God, we should carry ourselves decently and virtuously, living by godly standards. Walking in (real) love is having the disposition that can only come from God. That disposition will give you the *right motives* to attract the *right man*!

All a man's ways seem innocent to him; but motives are weighed by the Lord.
Proverbs 16:2

The enemy tells single women that it's only the outer appearance that matters, and if you do things like lose weight, have long hair (whether it's yours or store-bought), and dress provocatively then you can get a good man. Not true. I've been there and done all of that; I only attracted exactly what I was— *superficial men*. I'm not saying that we shouldn't take care of ourselves, but if your motive is to get a man, you are in for a disappointment.

Always check your motives and make sure they come from a pure and honest place in your heart, not from a position of trying to manipulate or deceive a man. Remember your motives are weighted by God, and you cannot fool Him! The *only* way to receive what *He* has for you is to have good intentions in all that you do!

Did you know that Flirting can hinder your Love Walk?

We use our eyes/body language to convey what our intentions are. Love is not having any lustful or ungodly intentions. Some women do things like wink their eyes, switch their hips, blow kisses, and hack up their skirts to get a man's attention. These things send mixed signals and cause confusion, which could take us back to the wilderness (think of virtue, ladies)!

Many women don't realize it, but, when you flirt with men in that way you open yourself up to judgment. A godly man will see that type of flirting as spiritual immaturity and a worldly man will immediately be attracted to you.

Ladies, you must realize that worldly men want worldly women!

So, ask yourself, "Do I want a man that has the character of God or the character of Satan?"

After reading the *characteristics of love* and knowing God is love, I certainly want a man that resembles God. Also, once you and God become joined at the hip, you will only desire a man with a godly nature. You will possess that nature as well and it will attract the right person!

We need to treat *every* man with the same loving characteristics even if we *are* attracted to him. Always let a man pursue you (make the first move) and **save** your flirting for the "Right" man!

A. Renee Wilson

The love you find in that "right person" is the beginning of your adventure with them. Over time, it grows into something much deeper than just a relationship. You develop a bond that cannot be broken, kindred that cannot be explained, and a love that will never end!

Chapter 7
The Schizophrenic Soul

Have you ever been hooked on a man that was not good for you, and you couldn't figure out why? Or is there a man from your past that you haven't seen for years but still have feelings for?

The reason you have these feelings is because you have a soul-tie to them that only God can break! When a man enters your heart and mind through having a relationship with him, that's when the soul connection is made. It doesn't matter if it was for two months or two years, the soul connection is there.

During sexual intercourse, women are the receivers; and when a man *physically* enters her, the flesh connection is made. It's a double-tied knot in our physical body/flesh and our mind/soul!

That's the reason you still desire him and will often think about him. If you've lain with several different men and had relationships with them, then you have soul ties to *all* of them! Sounds scary, right? And you wonder why you are so messed up inside when it comes to men.

These soul ties create a "schizophrenic soul" within you that the enemy absolutely loves. This "schizophrenic-soul" makes it difficult for you to distinguish between what is real and unreal, think clearly, manage emotions, and relate to others.

The wilderness search has all the characteristics of schizophrenia— confusion, emotional mood swings, and the building of walls/not trusting.

The schizophrenic soul acts up by having you compare the *new man* in your life with one of your *old men*. It will have you seeking a man with *all* the qualities you like from different men— you know, building your perfect man. When you begin to understand that *there is no perfect man,* you'll stop making it hard for a man to please you.

The restlessness of the schizophrenic soul makes it very difficult for you to relate to *any* man, because you have all these different men floating around in your head!

Another thing it will do is act up after a breakup. When we feel lonely, these are the times we are the most vulnerable. That's when we start to think about ex-boyfriends, and out of desperation we may call them and even make plans to see them. Going back to an ex can be a huge mistake!

When you go back, you open up all the old wounds and create new ones. It's like being released from prison, then opening the jail cell and going back voluntarily! I know that sounds absurd, but realize this, ladies— the same reason you broke up with him the first time will be the same reason you break up with him the second or third time. Most women go back because of a sense of familiarity, which is really an excuse not to deal with their issues.

I challenge each of you to take a step of faith and allow God through His grace to destroy your soul ties before even considering having a man in your life. Believe me, it won't be easy to reflect on your past relationships, but by this point you have gained a lot of strength and are ready to be totally set free!

The Soul-Tie Break Challenge!

- Write down the names of every man you have been involved with on a piece of paper (remember forgiveness is the key to healing).

- Delete emails, phone numbers and text messages (completely remove all physical evidence of them)!

- Pray out loud; ask God to break every soul-tie by calling out each one of their names and declare that you no longer have a soul-tie to them in the name of Jesus (throw away the list)!

- Receive your deliverance by faith, thank and Praise God!!

When your soul ties are broken, believe it—forever! Believe it and speak it, bring it to pass in your life.

Death and life are in the power of the tongue, and they who indulge in it shall eat the fruit of it [for death or life].
Proverbs 18:21

There will be times when you will have to speak out loud that you have no more soul ties, because the enemy will try to trick you and make you think you're not delivered. We have the power to destroy or build our lives with the words we say. When we talk about our present or future, we must speak positively by faith to release that over our lives. Please do not commit *spiritual suicide* by talking negative about yourself like, "I will never be married nor have children," or "I am always going to be broke," or "I am never going to get over this man." That type of thinking and talking will only lead to a life full of despair; you are basically saying to God that you don't believe Him.

The action of speaking your deliverance brings life and power to it. Remember, it's not about our will but God's grace that gives us the ability to stand. The magnificent thing about it is that you are changing your desires by "renewing your mind!" Before you know it, you will not even think about those men, and you will not desire to feed the flesh in this area of your life!

The last man I dated in the wilderness was everything my flesh desired. He was six feet six, financially stable, very handsome, and charismatic (I told you the enemy knows what we like)! The enemy pulled out all the guns for this man. He was my physical and spiritual Goliath! There were so many times I tried to stop seeing him, but the soul tie kept me bound to him. In my mind, we were in a *good* relationship because we talked every day and dated each other regularly. Once he had me where he wanted me, he started saying he didn't want a commitment with any woman; he wanted to have his cake and eat it too.

Eventually, I started to feel used and foolish, that's when I asked God to break the tie to him because I truly wanted to be set free. God did it. I stopped talking to him as much, and when I did talk to him, I ministered to him about God changing me. Months later, God used the same man to confirm the soul tie was truly broken.

One night he called me and wanted me to come over. I stood my ground and told him that I had no desire to see him like that anymore. The next morning, he called me and said, "I'm proud of you and I respect you as a God-fearing woman with a pure heart" (his exact words)! He also said that he could no longer be a negative influence in my life and that he was going to make some decisions in his life to honor God.

Once God delivers you from all your soul ties, you are pure and free but be aware that the enemy will make an announcement in hell that you are pure again. That's why it's extremely important to stay true to your boundaries and keep your guard up.

The enemy knows that sexual intercourse is one of the main gates to pollute you again, so he and his partners will try everything they can to get you back. Even dating broken men in the church could contaminate you again. We must hold *all* men accountable to our values.

Man~kation Tip 14: "Celibacy Equals Confidence!"

There is a confidence in knowing the enemy can no longer use the tactic of *sex* against you. This confidence will keep you walking in the Spirit with your chest out. Your mind is set on knowing *only* your God-sent husband is deserving of an intimate relationship with you. Saving yourself for the man whom God says is worthy of not only making love to your body, but also to your soul and spirit, builds tremendous reassurance and anticipation within you!

Anytime your flesh acts up in this area, you will immediately know that you've already won *that* battle, so it will be easy to keep it moving!

Man~Kation

Now that you are this mature woman in Christ, it's time to act like it, speak like it, and be like it. God has given you this thick skin, and you have no soul ties to any man. Now you can receive your God-given man with a virtuous soul, where *only* he will dwell!

Now you *can* distinguish between what is real and unreal, you *can* think clearly, you *can* manage emotions, and you *can* relate to others!

No more "schizophrenic-soul!

Chapter 8
Killing Your Ego

This bad ego thing was another *big* mountain I had to climb during my man-kation. I came from a family of two very strong-willed grandmothers. Both were outspoken and known for their tenacity. My maternal grandmother's family was known for being bold, bigheaded, and hostile. I grew up watching them and had other female family members with the same characteristics.

By the time I was in my twenties, I had the same attitude. I spoke my mind and didn't care if someone liked me or not. To me, it was representing them. I was told growing up not to let anyone disrespect me and to speak up for myself. There is nothing wrong with speaking up for yourself, but my problem was that I was young and hurting, so I did it out of pride, ego, anger, and insecurity.

I had a better-than-you attitude. I thought because I had money, lived in a big house, and drove a Mercedes, that I could look down on others. I was very judgmental and could always find fault in other people but never myself. I would brag about what my husband bought me, knowing that our marriage had issues. I lived a very superficial life and felt like if I inflated myself above other people, I would feel better.

The more I did this, the more isolated I became. Pride and ego were working together to keep me defeated. I had few friends and strife with family members. One of my uncles and I didn't speak to each other for years because of an argument over who was right about something. God would later show me myself in the situation and put my ego in check.

Once God turned on the light by humbling me through my trials and tribulations, I learned that was not a "real" way of living—it was only a phony life that kept me trapped in a world of perplexity. I was walking around with my noise in the air on the outside but hurting deeply on the inside.

Nothing outside a person can defile them by going into them. Rather, it is what comes out of a person that defiles them.

Mark 7:15

Jesus says it so plain in this scripture that we cannot blame people or the devil; it's what we say and do that makes us defiled.

The *ego* is an *arrogant/negative emotion* that is wrapped around our insecurities. It causes us to try to build ourselves up to be more than we should, which leads to self-pride!

Our negative emotions get us into a lot of trouble by making us act like a child to a situation instead of using godly wisdom. God is a spirit and emotions are not a part of who He is, so to emulate Him we should strive to walk in the Spirit!

Why do we continue to act on our emotions when their track record shows they are unstable, untrustworthy, and unrealistic? Selfishness. The ego has a way of making us feel superior to others and tremendously builds up our flesh! It's constantly concerned with "what I deserve" (prerogative) and "how people see me" (it's all about me)! Pride/Ego is always about looking out for number one.

Some selfish thoughts are

- "Who does he think he is (by not calling me back)? When he does call back, I'm not going to answer!"
- "I don't need anyone. I can take care of myself!"
- "Love doesn't live here anymore; it's all about me getting what I want!"

Some of you might say, "I don't have a bad ego," or "I don't have those kinds of thoughts," Okay, let's look at some aspects of the ego and what causes them.

Bad Attitudes

Telling people off, rage, backbiting, gossip, belittling people, and thinking negative. This comes from an unforgiving spirit, being mad at yourself, being full of regret, being mad at others, and not willing to take responsibility for your actions.

Impatience

Wanting everything now, wanting everything to come easy, not willing to work or wait for anything, immaturity, and laziness. This comes from a spirit of entitlement— "I deserve what I want now."

Never Satisfied

Always wants more, wanting what someone else has, jealousy, upset about your shortcomings but won't do anything to change them. This is caused by a spirit of greed and dissatisfaction.

Loud/Bossy

Controlling, always right, wanting everything your way, and always having the last word. This is caused by an un-submissive and undisciplined spirit.

Man~kation Tip 15:
"Will the Real You Please Stand Up?"

The heart of the wise inclines to the right, but the heart of the fool to the left.
Ecclesiastes 10:2

The fake and fantasy life is driven by a big ego and is completely to the left! This is an exceedingly foolish lifestyle that leads to self-esteem issues and can cause debt. It is a very sad way of living when you can't just be yourself.

Women wear a mask of what they think a man wants and performs by telling lie after lie. This causes the man to become confused about her, which can lead to many problems in their relationship. Some women even go into debt by trying to keep up with other women. They spend enormous amounts of money on shoes, jewelry, clothes, etc.— things that they really cannot afford!

The fact is that most women in the wilderness have completely bought into the devil's lie that there is a "shortage of good men." Thus, they play dating games that everyone who is single in the wilderness says is a part of being single. Wilderness women try to act like men by playing these games but end up losing—*big time*!

Food for thought!

The wilderness is truly "a man's world." He is the master at playing games because he wrote the rules. Now that's something to ponder!

God did not design us to live in the confusion of trying to act one way but think another. Today's psychology calls that bipolar. Playing dating games is a complete disorder and an ignorant way of living— especially for women— because *we never win*!

Another issue with fakeness is that we want to be people-pleasers (justified by people). The devil deceives women into thinking that people will accept them only if their insecurities are covered up. So, they create a facade to cover up the real person, hoping they will be accepted. This fakeness causes them to lie to themselves and start to become completely unaware of the truth.

The fake wilderness woman's thoughts are

- "It's ok for me to dress like I'm in my twenties even though I'm in my late thirties."
- "I know I can't afford this $500 purse, but I'm going to buy it anyway to keep up my image!"
- "The only reason they don't like me is because I've got what they want!"

I also found that the wilderness woman can't be real friends with other women because the competition is so high! There is a fear that her friend might have more money, more education, or may have better looks. This causes us to be isolated from other women, which is exactly what the enemy wants.

The fact is that we need each other to relate to and to help get through our issues.

Another fake thing that some women do is get fake breasts, buttocks, eyes, and hair. There again, ladies, I'm not saying that you shouldn't do those things, but just keep it real with yourself and check your motives. Are you trying to attract men, or do you want to enhance the beauty you already have?

Remember God knows our *real intentions* and wants us to completely turn away from the "left" (fake) life to the "right" (real) life He has for us! Praise the Lord that we belong to a confident, self-approved God and are not of the world system of trying to please people. We should strive to please God through our spirit (the real you) *not* our emotions, pride or ego!

These six things the Lord hates, indeed, seven are an abomination to Him: [17]A proud look [the spirit that makes one overestimate himself and underestimate others], a lying tongue, and hands that shed innocent blood.
Proverbs 6:16-17

Ego is hypocritical and false glamor, and the Lord hates it! In God's eyes, a prideful person has even exalted himself above Him. Your ego will keep you living a conquered life and is the reason you can't have productive relationships with anyone, including yourself.

A lying tongue is mentioned twice in this passage, that's why I say it's very important that you stay true to yourself while you are on your man-kation.

Ego will have you thinking that everything is okay, but you may be lonely, confused, and living in denial about the truths in your life. Staying truthful is the only way *real* transformation will take place. Lying is a way of covering up hurt, but *truth* heals hurt and protects you from returning to your fake life!

Man~kation Tip 16:
"Be his lover, not his mother!"

The foolish woman is noisy; she is simple and open to all forms of evil, she [willfully and recklessly] knows nothing whatever [of eternal value].
Proverbs 9:13

Did you know that your ego and bad attitude could be the reason you *don't* have a man? Our ego causes us to try to change a man instead of changing ourselves. Our ego makes us bossy, and we try to completely take charge of a man. We tell a man how he should behave, dress, and try to choose his friends. There's nothing wrong with giving him advice on those things, but when we do it to control him because of what *we* want, that's out of order.

A controlling woman is driven by her fears of being alone. She thinks that if she controls a man that she will keep him, when, the man will start to resent her and end up leaving or cheating on her to regain his self-respect.

We have to accept a man for who he is when we meet him. Being loud and bossy pushes him away. We must respect and love men as adults and not belittle them with insults, comparisons to other women's husbands, or even to our fathers. Men want to feel valued, needed, and admired by their woman. They will probably never tell us this, but they need these things.

Another problem is when we get into a relationship with a man, we become displeased because we start to evaluate him from day one. We keep a check on things we dislike about him instead of focusing on his good qualities. We are never satisfied with a man, because we put too many expectations (our fantasy again of the perfect man) on him. When he doesn't live up to our fantasy of how a man should treat us, he is all of a sudden, a bad man. Remember, we need to make sure that we focus on his *qualities* and not *our fantasy*!

It's important to focus on the *right* things about him, the *right* reasons you chose him, and the *right* relationship you want to develop with him! So many times, people fall out of love, because they forget to focus on the *right* things and inflate the *wrong* things. Relationships take a lot of work, so when you deem them to be *right* for you, make sure you're ready to put in the work!

Let's get ourselves together first so we can be our husbands' lovers and not their mothers, then let God be in control of any changes that are needed. God showed me the reason we act this way is because of our past hurts, which makes us build up a *protection shield of pride* that says, "I'm not going to let another man hurt me, use me, or disrespect me," This type of thinking causes some women to think that they don't need a man—they have the I-can-take-care-of-myself mentality—but as soon as they realize they are all alone, they desire to have one.

Having a husband is much more than just having someone to take care of you. It is a lifetime partnership, friendship, and *connection of love* that you will not experience with any other human on earth!

Fighting this war with your ego can become very difficult. But God wants us to rely on His grace and have a fighter mentality to obtain victory! You may get bumps and bruises, but you can't give up.

I always think of God, Jesus, and the Holy Spirit as my support team— my coach, my mentor, and my drill sergeant. I can always retreat (thru prayer, the Word and worship) to them to regain my strength and go back and fight *any* battle victoriously!

6 helpful tips to killing your ego

1. Humble yourself. *It's not always about you!* Ask God to forgive you and show you how to stop being self-seeking and un-submissive.
2. Accept yourself (stop the fakeness). You are "fearfully and wonderfully created by God" (Psalm 139:14). Love every aspect about yourself, the good and the bad!
3. Change how you see single men. Focus on the godly qualities in a man, not superficial things.
4. Accept others for who they are. We are all different! That is the marvelous creative thing about God; He does not exalt one child

over the other. Your acceptance of others will also help you to accept yourself.

5. Stop the LOVE of money. There is nothing wrong with being financially wealthy, but do not let that be your main focus in life. There is no need to impress or compete. *Focus on being "spiritually wealthy" and then it will manifest in the physical!*
6. Stay connected to Jesus. Always consider Jesus in every thought and action. Ask yourself, w*hat would Jesus do or say*?

Those tips will help you to be set free from your ego. When you control your attitude, you gain latitude!

After all you can never be a champion without a battle, so choose to WIN the battle of killing your ego!

Chapter 9
Leave Your Baggage in The Wilderness

In the previous chapters of this book, I described the different bags that women carry. In this chapter, I will discuss a few major ones God showed me. Some of us carry more than others, but we all have them in the wilderness.

The fact is we can only run for so long with the bags, but then the weight becomes so heavy that we give up and go back to old ways. God wants us to live freely in Him with no guilt, no weights, and nothing holding us down.

Condemnation Bag

One of the biggest bags is *condemnation*. God showed me a lot of women have issues with condemnation. We condemn ourselves every time we have a pity party. I call it the "should've-could've-would've syndrome!" We say, "I should've done this…or could've done that…"

We ask God why this or that happened, or why can't we have this or that. Then we start to blame God, which is exactly what the devil wants us to do.

"God didn't choose that man you regret marrying; so, stop pestering Him about the divorce!"

"God didn't make you eat all those donuts, so stop complaining to Him about your clothes not fitting!"

We complain and maintain regret, and it all leads to pity parties!

Man~kation Tip 17: "Pity parties are pathetic!"

My pity parties would start when something did not go my way or if I saw someone with something I used to have or wanted. I would go into this should've-could've-would've zone, which caused me to be negative and hopeless. The thoughts consumed my mind so much that I would go back to my bad behavior and feeling distraught!

The longer I stayed in the pity party, the more baggage I picked up. I was still in the world's way of thinking, looking at every situation in my life as some sort of punishment for my sins. I was holding myself accountable for the punishment and kept piling on the bags by saying, "I will never get it right. I keep doing the same thing over and over." I asked God to forgive me so many times, but I was not receiving His forgiveness. This goes back to chapter 4 when I talked about forgiving yourself and others, so you *can* receive God's forgiveness.

I wanted to give up so many times. I thought, *"If God really loves me, then why do I keep going through so much pain? Will I ever get the peace and joy I want for my life?"*

I didn't trust myself because of the baggage. I was trying to receive my freedom, but the bag of condemnation kept holding me back. I couldn't let it go because it was a part of me for so long. This happened off and on in my life for years. Even though I was saved, I hadn't received what the Word said about condemnation and that Jesus justified me.

> *THEREFORE, [there is] now no condemnation (no adjudging guilty of wrong) for those who are in Christ Jesus, who live [and] walk not after the dictates of the flesh, but after the dictates of the Spirit. ²For the law of the Spirit of life [which is] in Christ Jesus [the law of our new being] has freed me from the law of sin and of death.*
>
> Romans 8:1-2

Jesus paid the price for our freedom of past regrets, mistakes, hurts, and *condemnation*. The word says that there is *no* condemnation of sin to those that believe in Jesus Christ *and* walk after the Spirit in godly wisdom. I was saved, but my mind was carnal. I was living based on what I could see, hear, or touch. I had to learn how to live in the *spirit of my mind* and not the *feelings of my mind*.

Did you know that you can choose your thoughts?

From the time we wake up until we go to sleep, our minds are continuously presented with thoughts. We must choose which ones to believe and act on. It's very important that you "think about what you're thinking about"! Don't just let some idle, idiotic, thought hang around in your head; cancel it and remain focused on guarding/choosing your thoughts!

Guarding your thoughts is crucially important to learning how to live in the spirit of your mind. Our thoughts must always be based on the spiritual things by faith of what God says we shall have, who we are, and what we shall do. Controlling our thoughts by keeping them on the things above heavenly things changes our perspective and desires. Then you will really be led by your spirit and not your flesh, which keeps you out of condemnation—bag dropped!

One of my favorite Evangelists says, "Where the mind goes the man follows." This is very true. If your mind tells you that you're a failure and can't make any good decisions, either you will sit and do nothing or continue to make decisions based on your emotions. Guarding your thoughts comes from the boundaries you set (through godly wisdom) that we talked about in "Walking in Wisdom". This boundary is the "fence" that keeps you out of the wilderness-mindset.

Guarding your thoughts requires commitment, which takes a sacrifice (at first)—giving up something to stay true to your boundaries. Continue to pull down strongholds (negative thoughts) and replace them with positive thoughts *daily* according to 2 Corinthians 10:4. This takes time and dedication just like when you set a goal to lose weight or start exercising. In the beginning, you will think it's too hard, but the more you keep pursuing your goal the easier it becomes.

When you start to reap the rewards from your commitment, you will admit it was definitely worth the sacrifice, and it becomes easier for you to do.

<u>Low Self-Esteem Bag</u>

Wisdom informed me that a man's actions are truly what he is!

One of the many things that men in the wilderness do is lie. They lie about how they feel about you, where they want the relationship to go, or about you being the only woman they are interested in. I know this from personal experiences and from hearing the stories of women around me. Believing those lies causes so many disappointments and anger, but the truth of the matter is his *actions* are who he is, not his *words*.

We must focus on a man's actions to see if they line up with what he says. The saying "talk is cheap" is true, but actions are priceless! When we are constantly lied to, it makes us feel less than good enough to deserve the truth. This can destroy our self-image and causes us to judge *every* man as a liar.

I just didn't want to get to the point where I couldn't believe any man or hated men, so I had to take a man-kation to get a better perspective of them.

Knowing your own self-worth is crucially important to restoring your self-esteem. You are created in God's image (Genesis 1:27) and are worthy of receiving only His best! One of your boundaries in dating will definitely be to set the standard of how *you* want to be treated by a man. We will talk about the distinction between a godly man and a wilderness man later in this book.

Just know that once our self-esteem is restored then we can clearly recognize the difference between the two types of men. This helps us to understand that the rejection and the breakups were a part of living in the wilderness. Once we realize the wilderness experiences had to happen, then we can appreciate where God has brought us from and is taking us to!

Man~kation Tip 18:
"Impatience causes Impulsive Behavior!"

Impatience Bag

Another big bag we carry is the *impatience bag*. This was a huge bag I had to drop. I would go for so long saying I'm going to wait on God, and then out of impatience I would do something impulsive, which would lead me back to the wilderness.

About four months into my man-kation I wasn't dating anyone but was feeling lonely; and the more I tried to focus on God the more my flesh was acting out. It would wake me up at night and try to bring back memories or try to evaluate different men I dated to see which one would be safe to call and just to have a "conversation" with. So, one weekend, I called an old acquaintance. I thought that he was safe because we had only been on two dates. The phone conversation led to dinner, and before I knew it, I was back to my old way of thinking (no intimacy), but the more I focused on this man that I knew was not for me, the more I drifted from God.

My emotions were slowly pulling me away from God. My spirit kept warning me because there was no peace about him. I wasn't really attracted to him, and he was only there because of one moment of impatience, which led to opening the door to impulsive behavior, which led to my flesh being fed by this man's attention. Once my flesh was fed it started to take over with compromising thoughts and concerns about not hurting the man's feelings.

For a righteous man falls seven times and rises again, but the wicked are overthrown by calamity.
Proverbs 24:16

After that "stumble on the road", I had to ask God to forgive me for allowing someone space in my head that was not reserved for them. The Word says that a righteous man falls but continues to rise. God knows all our shortcomings. He understands we are humans, and because of what Jesus went through, He can relate to our humanity. The dedication God requires of us is to continue to stay humble knowing that we *will* make mistakes, but His grace covers us. God has already *fully* committed to us when He gave His son to die for us. We must commit to Him by acknowledging our faults, His grace, and then stay in the race!

Man~kation Tip 19:
"Past baggage is Trash—clean your house!"

When we carry bags and meet a man, we want him to accept all our trash, so we dump it on him and expect him to just deal with it. God showed me that the men, too, are on a journey and carry bags of trash as well, but His sons are not a trash dump, and neither are we!

In the wilderness, men and women carry these trash bags into a relationship, throw their bags together, and then expect something good to come out of the relationship. Trash on top of trash is nothing but trash! Nothing pleasant, safe, prosperous, or godly comes from trash!

Your man-kation time is your cleanup time. So, get rid of all the trash in your house. You are moving to a new house; a mansion in your abundant life that Jesus promised you. If you bring your bags (old way of thinking/acting) to your new mansion, it's like putting old/broken furniture in a brand-new house.

Having a clean house is a house that is free from pain, regrets, ego, lust, and selfishness. God has your new life in the mansion on the hill that is above all your past mistakes and hurt. It is beautiful, pure, restored, full of happiness, and love.

Just imagine how sweet it will be when you meet your man and he comes into your clean house, free from trash; a pleasant house that has the spirit of God and is built on solid ground, not a fantasy of perfection, but" perfecting," which is the closest thing to perfection!

Man~kation Tip 20:
"Wait on your Man—Expect God's Best!"

My soul, wait only upon God and silently submit to Him; for my hope and expectation are from Him.
                                                      Psalm 62:5

Okay, ladies, now that your house is clean, wait patiently for your baby (your man). Don't ask God when he will come, just believe that He is preparing the *best* man for you! Think about it this way: When a woman finds out she's pregnant and the doctor gives her the due date, only God knows when the baby will be born. During the pregnancy, a woman takes extra good care of herself by going to all her doctor's appointments; she buys baby clothes and baby furniture. She is getting ready for her baby even though she hasn't seen the baby yet. She prays for a healthy baby and believes that God will answer her prayers.

Do the same things for your expectant man (your baby). Take the time to pamper yourself. Get busy *"buying furniture"*; meaning, eat right, exercise, get your finances in order, go back to school, get your pedicures/spa treatments. "Buy clothes"— dress yourself in clothes that make you feel and look good. You represent a *prosperous* God, and He wants you to be prosperous.

I'm not only talking about physical things but spiritual as well, so make sure you "Keep your doctor appointments with God"— pray, meditate, read and hear the Word (get your medicine), knowing that you are stronger, wiser, and so much better than you were before you took your mankation! God *is* determined to give you what you desire and that's His best!

Then, when God delivers him to you, make sure that you continue to keep yourself clean on the inside and out. Don't get complacent and think that you don't have to keep yourself up or do all the things you did before you got him. *What got the man will keep the man,* and the things I'm asking you to do, is not just for him, but it is for you too!

God's grace is full of unlimited blessings!

God is the same. He is always there waiting for you to surrender all to him so He can do extraordinary things in your life. He doesn't bless people based on favoritism; He blesses based on faith by His grace (unmerited favor)!

As I continued my man-kation, I finally decided that I'm not going to let anything from my past hold me back. I'm going to surrender *all my bags* to God. That is when my deliverance took place, surrendering all (*wanting* to be completely delivered) to God and not trying to change in my own ability. Then God gave me strength to do His will through the Holy Spirit in me. One day, I heard a message preached about God's grace. I realized that God really does empower me and that I don't have to carry my bags anymore.

When you drop your bags and walk in the Spirit, the blessings of God will overtake you. You have happiness and a hope in God that no one can take from you. This happiness will flow to everyone and everything around you. This is the carefree/stress-free life we all desire to have.

Finally appreciate this; that in God's kingdom you will *never* have to carry another bag, because you are treated like the royal princess that you are. When the cares of this life come up, you will immediately know to give your bags to God, and He will take care of them for you.

This makes me think about traveling in an airport. There is a skycap to help you with your bags, but you *must* allow him to help.

Drop your bags today, ladies, and "take flight" to receive all that God has for you!

Chapter 10
Enter God's Garden by Faith

My Garden Time Testimony

When I first got saved, I was on fire for the Lord, going to church anytime the church doors were opened. I truly fell in love with Jesus! Those years I flourished in knowledge. Even though I grew up in a "traditional" Baptist church, as an adult, to develop a "real" relationship and a "real" love for Jesus was awesome!

As an "adolescent" in Christ, I started to struggle. Those were the lesson years! In my mid- thirties, my relationships and finances were beginning to struggle. My marriage was destroyed, I was in debt, eventually I began to backslide, and going back to the clubs became part of my life again.

As I talked about early, I experienced a lot of hurt from my past, and my attitude was very bad. Even though I was in a backslidden state, I could still hear God calling me to come out.

One day, I decided to obey God and started going back to church. This was the start of my man-kation. God took me to His Garden and kept me there. My man-kation showed me that what was happening to me was a process of s*piritual maturity*. God was stretching me to be more like Him for my next-level assignment. The stretching was required to get all of the "worldly junk" out of me. God knew what it would take to get me to really look at myself and not try to make excuses or ignore my issues.

In the Garden, I started each day with personal devotion time. In the morning, I woke up early and got on my knees and prayed. I read one scripture and then meditated on it throughout the day. In the car on the way to work I sang praise and worship unto God. In the midst of all that, God warned me against things for the day and encouraged me. I loved having so much insight. The Holy Spirit kept me on top of things.

One morning, while I was on my man-kation, God showed me the different relationships I had between Him as the Father and Jesus as the son. When I first got saved, I fell in love with Jesus through the confession of Him as my savior; my focus was on Him and God seems far off. God showed me that I had to fall in love with His son first, to get to Him.

My garden time revealed to me that falling in love with Him was agape love! It's that deep spiritual love that takes you to the next level. I can now see and fully accept the love He has for me and all His children. I no longer see Him as some far-off God, but I see Him as my "Abba-Father" whom I can count on.

When you're in the garden, oh my, what a revelation time it will be for you! There was a peace that fell over me that I can't fully explain. I started to rest in Him—everyday, all day. In my physical life there were many things trying to stop me from entering into God's garden, but I pressed every day to get there! Because I knew the longer, I stayed there the more content I became.

The LORD is my shepherd; I shall not want.²He maketh me to lie down in green pastures: he leadeth me beside the still waters.³He restoreth my soul: he leadeth me in the paths of righteousness for his name's sake.
Psalm 23:1-3

Picture God's Garden—a paradise with calming waters, green pastures, and vibrant flowers. This is a peaceful place where there's only you and God; your time to love on Him and for Him to love on you. God wants to restore you and fill you completely with His spirit.

This garden is your path to His righteousness. Growing in the things of God leads you into right standing with Him. When you're firmly planted in the garden, He makes you rest there, so He can produce all the fruits of His spirit in you.

Now faith is the substance of things hoped for, the evidence of things not seen.
Hebrews 11:1

Our personal "retreat time" with God is precious, so please visit it *daily*! Not everyone can go to God's garden; only by *faith* can you receive your ticket!

Faith takes you from the *wilderness* to the *garden—instantly*! When that *"faith-superglue connection"* is made, it brings forth change, hope, wisdom, and a confidence in God like never before! Spiritually, you will be at peace in your father's arms. God is hope. You cannot see Him, but by *faith* you can feel Him and rest in His Garden.

In the spirit, by faith, you can *always* retreat to God's Garden— your resting place. In this time of meditation, prayer and faith are working together to build your security in God. He has *everything* in control; you will *not* worry again (if you trust and believe). The things that used to bother you will no longer bother you; your motives start to change; your desires start to change—you change!

A. Renee Wilson

For the Lord will comfort Zion; He will comfort all her waste places. And He will make her wilderness like Eden, and her desert like the garden of the Lord. Joy and gladness will be found in her, thanksgiving and the voice of song or instrument of praise.

                                                      Isaiah 51:3

I love when this scripture says, "He will make your wilderness like a Garden of Eden, your desert the garden of the Lord." There He gives you joy like you never had before. He builds your self-esteem to resemble Him. This place gives you so much confidence in God's qualities, that it cleanses you, wipes away your tears and creates in you a clean heart (Psalm 51:10). God reveals Himself to you; and when you give Him praise and thanksgiving, He fellowships with you!

It is the best vacation spot in the *universe*! And guess what—Jesus has already paid the price for your admittance!

God has destined Men and Women to bond together in His Garden!

When God created Adam, He saw that it was not good for him to be alone and that he needed a "suitable" helper (Genesis 2:18). A single man is unbalanced if he doesn't have "suitable" support from a "wise" woman. Likewise, a woman without the covering and leadership of a "godly" man is living in lack. One-half and one-half makes *one whole*, so you can be incomplete without your other half, but God has a plan to reconcile His daughters and sons in His garden!

Man~kation Tip 21:
"God has One Man Especially Created for You!"

Do you really believe that your *one* God-given man is already created and waiting for you? After spending time with God and building my trust in Him, I certainly do. I not only believe it, but I only desire that *one* man! We must enter His Garden to get completely equipped for that man and equipped for the next level in God! Just as God created Adam and put him in the garden, *our man* is also in the Garden waiting for us to reach the level of spiritual maturity where we will appreciate him, respect him, and *love* him!

Remember, God created man first and then He created the woman. We must be created into the virtuous woman that the Bible talks about in Proverbs 31. Our man-kation is our creation time!

Then Adam said, 'this [creature] is now bone of my bones and flesh of my flesh; she shall be called Woman, because she was taken out of a man,
Genesis 2:23

Men and women are destined to be together; this is something God intended from the beginning. In this scripture we see Adam proclaim we are "bone of his bone"; that means we are the supportive/sensible part of a man. He also said we are "flesh of his flesh"; we shall be attached to him as one, like white on rice! It is like two magnets; the bond is so strong that nothing can tear it apart, a "deep soul" connection that can be felt across continents!

That is the way God created it and that's the way it will be in a union that He has put together! That sounds too good to be true, right?

When God first showed me that scripture about Adam confessions regarding Eve, I didn't understand it. Now that He has given me *full* revelation, I will not settle for less than that. Remember, the enemy doesn't want you to be happy, so he will try to keep you doubting God's promise of a blessed marriage.

I certainly had my doubts, especially after my divorce, but the strange thing is that I grew up with an excellent example of what a blessed marriage looks like.

My paternal grandparents were married for close to fifty years and had a love connection that is really unexplainable. My man-kation reminded me of my grandparents' love. They truly adored one another. They were *always* together, holding hands and caring for one another. My grandmother told me that my grandfather was the best man God could have ever sent her. He was her second husband, so don't think a divorce will stop you from having a blessed marriage in your future!

Adam and Eve were the first husband and wife. He immediately claimed his woman and named her. That's the kind of man I desire; a man that knows who he is and what he wants. Now I know that I *must* have a man that is spiritually and emotionally strong!

The fact that you are seeking God by reading this book to get prepared is a step of faith, and God honors that. Please don't think for one moment that God has forgotten about you or that He wants you to be alone. He knows that two is much better than one, that's why He created Eve for Adam.

Ladies, believe that *you* were created for *one* extraordinary man. Now I want you to focus on your faith and consider this—*If there is a shortage of men, then God has your man already reserved for you in His Garden!*

Chapter 11
If you want a Boaz, You must be a Ruth

Now that we have left our bags in the wilderness and are in God's Garden, we are in a perfect position to become the Virtuous Women the Bible talks about. She is rare and hard for any noble man to find (Proverbs 31:10). She is more priceless than pearls or rubies. She is a woman that knows her self- worth and walks in wisdom, humility, love, and dignity.

There is an exceptional example in the Bible of a Virtuous Woman that possessed all of the characteristics that Proverbs 31 describes. Her name was Ruth, and she was the type of woman we should all strive to be. She received her special man (Boaz) not by anything she had on the outside but only by what she carried on the inside. God loved her so much that He dedicated a book in her name. Let's take a look at her story.

The book of Ruth tells a story about a widow that had nothing and only her mother-in-law Naomi, who was also a widow. Naomi had grown bitter and was lonely due to the death of both her husband and sons. Both women were in a wilderness, a place where they had experienced tremendous heartbreak— a dry place of death— their future seemed hopeless. God told them to leave their wilderness in search of something new.

Like Naomi and Ruth, we are also on a journey. This man-kation is an unknown place, somewhere we have never been before. God gave us the mandate to leave the wilderness and go to His garden, a new place of expectation for our future. Though many of us lost so much in the wilderness, God is going to do a new thing in us—in the Garden.

Ruth had to fight with Naomi from the beginning to go to the unknown land (Ruth 1:15-16), but when

Naomi saw that Ruth was determined to go, she agreed to let her come. I'm sure Ruth had some apprehension about going to an unknown land, but she activated her faith and was determined to obey God.

Always remember, when God tells you to do something the enemy will constantly come with opposition. That is confirmation that you are headed in the right direction.

So Naomi returned from Moab accompanied by Ruth the Moabite, her daughter-in-law, arriving in Bethlehem as the barley harvest was beginning.
Ruth 1:22

Stepping out on faith and moving when God says move is always the right timing. Naomi and Ruth arrived at the beginning of harvest season. This was the perfect time for Ruth to work in Boaz's fields.

Boaz was a very rich man that owned plenty of land and was well respected in the community. God knew exactly what He had planned for Ruth. She wasn't even looking for a husband, but Boaz was the man *God* chose for her.

Man~kation Tip 22:
Stop Dating "Broken Bobby" When God has "Blessed Boaz" waiting for You!

BLESSED BOAZ VS	BROKEN BOBBY
• Walks in the Spirit, satisfied with who he is in Christ, forgiving, patient, and speaks pleasantly to us, not disrespectful. • Transformed, confident, secure, walks in integrity & godly love! • Encouraging, ministers the Word of God using wisdom. • Lover, provider, prosperous, plans, comforting and generous.	• Walks in the flesh, dissatisfied, holds grudges, and lives for the moment. • Broken Spirit confused about spirituality or no desire to learn about God. • Discouraging, not willing to encourage because of pride and jealousy. • No love, selfish, no hope for the future, and roams from woman to woman.

"Blessed Boaz" is a man that is spiritually blessed and his lifestyle shows it. There is nothing broken about him because he totally leans on God and not his own ability. He has no problem talking about his relationship with God. He is a man that knows exactly who he is and what he expects from God concerning you.

"Broken Bobby," on the other hand, is a broken man that carries baggage from his childhood and/or other women. He is still in the wilderness and needs God for restoration from lust, pride, unforgiveness and trust. "Broken Bobby" will persistently try to pursue you. Because men are natural hunters and like the chase, he will find it hard to give up on the pursuit of you.

Wilderness men (Broken Bobby) are impulsive, inconsiderate, liars, cheaters, full of self-gratification and are *never* satisfied. Garden men (Blessed Boaz) are the exact opposite; they walk in godly love, are humble, and patient. You will definitely be able to recognize a garden man quickly by his actions, his words, and his lifestyle. He's not *perfect* but he is *pleasing* to your spirit!

I learned through godly wisdom to only trust what my spirit says deciphering between the two; meaning, *only* trust a man's spirit (his behavior). As you can see, there is a huge difference between "wilderness men" and "garden men". They display the attitudes of the place where they dwell.

There again ladies, it's very important to know your self-worth. Don't ever lower your value for a man that shows you his "bank statement" (his actions) that he cannot afford you. Keep it moving!

I love the way walking in the spirit keeps me from settling for less. I cannot tell you how many times I have heard from "Broken Bobby" that my standards are too high, or I act conceited. "Broken Bobby" always confuses our confidence (in God) with conceit, because he lacks wisdom and only thinks like the flesh. We know that God has not given us a spirit of arrogance but of humility. "Blessed Boaz" will see our self-confidence and also our humility and will appreciate it, because he too has that same uniqueness.

I want to emphasize that "Broken Bobby" can approach you in "Blessed Boaz" clothing. I don't care how much he talks about the Bible or even if he preaches the Word; if there is no peace in your spirit, don't settle for him.

Never ever settle for "Broken Bobby." Please wait for "Blessed Boaz."

Wait for the man who will be proud to say that you are his wife before he tries to make you spend a night!

Wait for the man who makes loving God a *priority* not a *preference*! If a man knows how to love God by embracing/obeying God, trusting God, and enjoying God then he will know how to embrace, trust, enjoy, and love you!

Wait for the man who has vision, not just for him but for the both of you!

Wait for Blessed Boaz. Please wait for him. Be patient. Wait for God to send your Prince Charming; he does exist, and remember he is waiting for you!

Ladies, we can help Broken Bobby transform into Blessed Boaz!

You may be thinking, why *do we want to help Broken Bobby*? Well, he is a part of the *male-species*— our goal is to save all our men (so we will have more to choose from)!

Just joking, but the truth of the matter is what kind of woman would we be if we only cared about the men who have made it out of the wilderness? That's not the kind of love God commands of us because there are plenty of "Broken Bobbies" in the church!

God gave us the power of persuasion. Let's reflect on Eve, the first woman. She was able to persuade Adam, the *very first man* whom God created! This woman was able to convince him to completely disobey *his* God. I wonder how she did it. No one really knows, but one thing is for sure, she undeniably had the power to influence him!

Now, we're *not* going to sway men in the wrong direction like Eve did, but you can see that we definitely have an influence over them. Men are strong physically and emotionally; however, *every* man has a weakness to the woman he loves.

We all *must* get on one accord *(a man-kation Movement)* and say, "I'm on a man-kation, so I will *not* sleep with you. I will *not* compromise and play games with you." Believe me, they will conform. Raising the bar of expectation *will* require *all* of them to meet that standard. They will resist at first, but if they want us (believe me, they do) they will come around.

The reason men get away with so much is because *we* allow it. If we close our legs and put our foot down by living like Ruth (in virtue), they will eventually be transformed into a "Blessed Boaz"!

"Blessed Boaz" wants "Restored Ruth", he won't settle for anything less.

A. Renee Wilson

Man~kation Tip 23:
A "Fruit-of-the-Spirit-Tree" You Must Be!

But the fruit of the Spirit is love, joy, peace, forbearance, kindness, goodness, faithfulness, [23] gentleness and self-control. Against such things there is no law.

Galatians 5:22-23

A man with a Boaz anointing can have any woman he wants, and he is continuously chased by women. However, he also has a standard of what he requires of his chosen wife. He won't accept anyone less than the woman God has put in his Spirit. God will *not* bring Blessed Boaz to a "broken" woman. She must be a restored woman to possess the fruit of the Spirit!

She is completely healed and loved by many because she walks in love. She is very hard for him to find (Proverbs 31:10) because many of us are so broken by our wilderness experiences that darkness fills our spirit. As I mention in the introduction, this man-kation is for the woman who is serious and willing to go "Through the Fire"— like Chaka Khan sang—to be transformed (purified like gold)! She will be the one that gets her Blessed Boaz!

The flesh and the spirit are constantly at war; they are complete opposites. We must strive to be steadfast, consistently producing all the fruit of the spirit. The previous chapters in this book gave us plenty of insight on how to produce these attributes.

The flesh tree is the exact opposite:

Now the doings (practices) of the flesh are clear (obvious): they are immorality, impurity, indecency, [20]Idolatry, sorcery, enmity, strife, jealousy, anger (ill temper), selfishness, divisions (dissensions), party spirit (factions, sects with peculiar opinions, heresies), [21]Envy, drunkenness, carousing, and the like. I warn you beforehand, just as I did previously, that those who do such things shall not inherit the kingdom of God.
Galatians 5:19-21

What type of tree are you? You cannot be one-half peach tree and one-half apple tree. I've never seen a tree that was one-half of one fruit and one-half the other. Your roots will show your fruit, so you must be all or nothing (Matthew 7:18).

A. Renee Wilson

Man~kation Tip 24: "Men of God want women that are Graceful!"

A graceful woman speaks with good judgment and kindness. She acts with good intentions and practices self-control. While she's not perfect, she should be *"perfecting"* those qualities.

Our Blessed Boaz has the same type of determination in his *"perfecting"* process. He only wants a woman that will resemble him and add *goodness* to his life.

Jesus said we must stay connected to Him to produce good fruit (John 15:4-6). Staying connected is to copy His temperament, His love, and His respect for God. If we don't then we shall surely fall and die. He also said that if we stay connected to Him whatever we ask *will* be given to us.

It's all about your moral fiber (your heart) to *not* act or think like the flesh, but to resemble Jesus! In a relationship with a man, again, your disposition is the foundation of your love walk with him. To remain in harmony, you must have the fruit of the spirit. I'm not saying there will not be issues in your relationship, but because you *both* are connected to the vine, you will immediately be able to forgive one another and deal with any issues.

There is no such thing as a *perfect* relationship but there is *perfecting*!

Perfecting to keep God in the center!
Perfecting to forgive immediately!
Perfecting to always be honest!
Perfecting to love unconditionally!

When you demonstrate the fruits of the spirit, your Boaz, led by the same Holy Spirit that leads you, will have no problem identifying who you are, respecting you, and loving you.

There will be a captivating radiance that glows around you and when you open your mouth to speak, your words will be like music to his ears. The sparkle in your eyes will connect with his, and he will immediately be drawn to you!

This man-kation helps us to constantly concentrate on the nature of God and how we should resemble it. The benefits of changing your mindset to God's will change every area of your life. You will become a better mother, daughter, sister, friend, employee, employer, and *Christian*!

Ruth was a woman that was kind, patient, gracious, and had self-control. Those attributes are hard to go unnoticed.

Ruth chapter 3 is very profound; please read the whole chapter to get a full understanding of how Ruth's obedience won over Boaz's heart. At the threshing floor— the place of change— Ruth shows the purity of her heart. She humbly slept at Boaz's feet and when he woke up, he saw her love and respect towards him and invited her to stay. They never got into the flesh or became intimate; because of her spirit, he promised to do everything he could to give her what she desired. After their encounter, Ruth went home and did exactly what Boaz and Naomi told her to do—wait.

You may have to wait a while for your Boaz, so don't be discouraged. This was enlightening to me, but I learned that this waiting period is to develop fruit to full maturity—your love walk, your patience. Remember love endures long!

While waiting, it's very important to be about God's work!

Man~kation Tip 25:
"Write a letter to your Boaz to stay on task!"

Writing letters to your Boaz during those times of "I'm about to give up," "I'm tired of being alone," "I want someone to hold me and whisper sweet nothings in my ear" are when we have to get out our notepad and start writing letters to our future. When your emotions are about to break, you need an escape! It's therapeutic. It gets you through. It gets you over the hump of wanting to give in to your emotions.

As you write your letters, you can be as detailed and personal as you want because they are love notes specifically for your future man!

I have a notebook full of letters to my Boaz and one day I will personally deliver them to him! My letters to him kept me from being distracted by my emotions and focused on God's promise of a blessed relationship!

I have so much expectation about what God is going to do in relationships between men and women. When two people that have a spiritual, soul, and physical connection are working for God's kingdom, what an amazing work they will do!

Miraculous things happen when a couple joins forces to fight the enemy, because where there is unity there is power! The enemy knows this and that is why he fights so hard to break up marriages and to keep women and men separated.

Your obedience to God is the *blueprint* to getting your Boaz. God gives specific instructions; listen,

listen—obey, obey! The longer you stay in disobedience the longer you stay single!

In Ruth Chapter 4, Boaz takes Ruth as his wife and she has a son named Obed; he was the father of Jesse, the father of King David (ancestor of Jesus Christ)!

God favored Ruth so much that two Kings came out of her lineage! By obeying God, who or what ministry will be birthed out of your lineage?

God knows! However, if you don't

Decide to change....
Decide to succeed....
Decide to Follow God.... you will *never* know!

Chapter 12
Pursue Your Purpose

Pursuing your purpose is to answer God's calling on your life. Your phone is ringing. Are you going to pick it up so that God can ignite something in you?

He will ignite a fire that is so intense that no doubt, no opinion, and no circumstances can put it out! A fire that goes into the very core of your being and will not let you be complacent anymore. A drive and a determination that you never had about anything before; a dream that will not go away!

The voice of God has been repetitively calling you. He needs you to operate for Him in the earthly realm to fulfill His purpose. He needs your mouth to speak His word and your hands to touch and heal. Will you answer the call that will not only save your life but the lives of others?

Man~kation Tip 26: "Live a life of Inspiration not Desperation!"

When you think about the things you have been through, just remember, God *will* use them for your assignment. The trials and tribulations are not about God repaying you for your sins, they are for the building of your testimony. The fact that you are an overcomer will inspire others to do the same.

For instance, if you have been on drugs or incarcerated, God can use you to minister to others in those situations. People want someone who has "walked in their shoes" and has triumphed to tell them how they overcame. God sent Jesus to be able to relate to us, and now He uses us to relate with others.

As you start to pursue your purpose, God will lead you every step of the way. Wisdom works continuously. I began to say to myself, "It's not about me but about my God-given assignment!" What a revelation it was for me to come to this contentment in my heart.

I began to comprehend that the struggles I experienced in relationships with men were all predestined by God. Once I answered the call, my spiritual eyes became open to the reasons I went through those struggles. Every question I had, He answered them through His wisdom with my purpose!

God knew He would use my testimony to help other women. I recognized that my life before I answered Him was full of perplexity. I was looking for answers in places that had no intellectual capacity for God's plan!

God said that my pain was my purpose in ministry!

Now that I understand why I went through so many things, I can say it was worth the pain and suffering. The process I had to endure built my strength and confidence in God! This book is a testament of God's purpose for my life. I give him *all the praise* for giving me the courage to write it. We are all put here on earth to do good works. After all, "faith without works is dead" (James 2:17-18).

God's divine purpose should be our main focus in life. "God, what can I do for you?" "What is your plan for me?" Every Christian should ask God those questions because He has an appointed future for us that must be fulfilled.

There are two ways to determine your God-given purpose. First, God *must* be in the center of it (to give Him the glory)! Second, it will be something that takes you out of your comfort zone; you will have to fully depend on Him to achieve it!

As you diligently seek God, He will unveil your purpose to you. Once God reveals this, your life will never be the same. I found myself being completely driven by purpose. I started to focus on living a life of inspiration to others instead of focusing on my selfish needs.

The more I focused on helping others, the more God changed me on the inside. I no longer wanted to keep living the life that I had lived for so long. My purpose consumed my thoughts; it woke me up in the middle of night and never let me settle for the ordinary life. The vision God gave me kept pushing me to stay focused on the "big picture" (my future) and not the small circumstances (my past or present) of my life.

There were times when I felt like giving up, but God reminded me of the story about Joseph during those moments. God gave Joseph a dream that he would be a powerful man (his purpose), but soon after the dream, he was thrown into a pit and sold into slavery (Genesis 37:9-27). Joseph had to keep believing that God doesn't lie, and His promises will come to pass, and we must do the same.

One night during my man-kation, I had a dream about a baby that was being eaten by a demon. The baby was lying on its side and crying faintly. I took a big sword out and cut off the demon's head, wrapped the baby in a blanket, and laid the baby on this huge altar. There was a bright light above the altar. I lay prostrate on the ground beneath the baby, crying and praying.

The dream had me shaken at first; the vision of cannibalism was so horrific. Then God said to me that the baby symbolized "my spiritual baby/my purpose" and every time I abandoned "my purpose/my baby," the enemy tried to kill it! God continued and said that I needed to see the spiritual importance and urgency of pursuing my purpose!

Ladies, I want you to always remember that we are soldiers in a spiritual war. Every soldier has a job that they must perform to fulfill the mission of God. Please do not take your Christianity lightly. It is our responsibility to do our part, to make sure the blood of other people is not on our hands. It is our job to tell others what we know and lead them to Christ.

> Why can people follow man's rules (jobs, policies, and procedures) for a paycheck, but cannot follow God's Word to reap His rewards?

But without faith it is impossible to please and be satisfactory to Him. For whoever would come near to God must [necessarily] believe that God exists and that He is the rewarder of those who earnestly and diligently seek Him [out].
Hebrews 11:6

The lack of faith is the reason; many people can *only* believe what they can see. Faith is all about believing what you cannot see and waiting for it to come to pass. Today's society is driven by the myth that "you have to see it to believe it." Many people rely on tangible things instead of living by faith. This makes them unable to not only see their God-given purpose but to believe it as well. God's rewards are eternal, and the things here on earth are temporary!

Another issue is that our culture wants everything to happen instantaneously! They may get the vision but are not willing to be patient and let *God's* map for their life play out. God showed me our lives in comparison to a treasure map. We, as believers, start our journey on the day of our salvation. Once we are saved, we are immediately covered by the blood of Jesus; He is the only way to salvation. We walk through twists and turns, mountains and valleys in our lives, and at every turn there is our spirit and our flesh that guides us to the left or right.

God already mapped out our lives and strategically placed us into the families, cities and ethnicities that we were born into. God knows everything we did do, are doing now, and will do in the future.

He has the *master plan* for our lives and knows every situation before we get to the road, but the decision of which way to turn is ours.

In all your ways know, recognize, and acknowledge Him, and He will direct and make straight and plain your paths.
                                    Proverbs 3:6

Consider this: When you are driving in an unknown area and you're looking for your destination, you take many turns only to find that your destination is just one *"right"* turn away! God will always lead you back to the right path. Don't try to figure everything out; just be led by faith and know that He has the steering wheel.

Confusion and distractions try to prevent you from seeing your purpose and to stop you, but God is determined to make sure you get it! He wants to give you insight, to answer all the questions in your life. When He speaks, the enemy must stop speaking; and remember God always speaks truthfully, positively, and lovingly.

God said that we all have spiritual gifts given from one Holy Spirit (1 Corinthians 12:1-5). These gifts were given to us in heaven (spiritual realm) before we entered into this earth realm. We are a spirit *first*, born into a body that possesses a soul.

Understanding that we are a spirit being "eternally" that lives in an earthly body "temporarily" helps us to tap into the Spirit easier. I had to recognize that the "facts of this world" are not the "facts of my spirit"; meaning, my life is dictated on what's in the spiritual realm (heaven)! God told me to stop talking about my feelings and to focus on the facts of my purpose!

The facts are from Genesis to Revelations. God has plainly put everything that our spirit needs to fulfill the reason He sent us here. The Bible is our training manual, so you must pick it up, read it, and study it to accomplish your purpose.

For God's gifts and His call are irrevocable. [He never withdraws them when once they are given, and He does not change His mind about those to whom He gives His grace or to whom He sends His call].
Romans 11:29

God's gifts are to help us finish the tasks He has given us. These gifts are our secret weapons to prove God's calling for our life. He does not take back what He has given us, so don't think that it's too late or that you have done so many bad things that God can no longer use you. He will *never* change His mind about you; He chose you from the foundation and has ordained a destiny for you that is far above what you can imagine!

Use your gifts *today* so that you can help change someone's life *forever*. People's souls are at stake.

Pursue your purpose with perseverance, patience, and power!

Chapter 13

The New You!

Therefore if any person is [engrafted] in Christ (the Messiah) he is a new creation (a new creature altogether); the old [previous moral and spiritual condition] has passed away. Behold the fresh and new has come!
                                        2 Corinthians 5:17

The new you *is* on the inside, and it now shows on the outside. You are no longer trying to be what people say you should be or what they say you're going to be. You are *only* who God says you are— a new creature! He has poured out His word, His spirit, and His love in your new vessel.

As you read every chapter in this book, a total transformation has been taking place that you probably didn't even realize, until you started to *believe* that it was written especially for you!

A. Renee Wilson

From a Caterpillar to a Beautiful Butterfly!

From a caterpillar to a butterfly was what God showed me in comparison to our transformation from the wilderness mindset to the garden mindset.

The butterfly goes through a complete metamorphosis, meaning that the adult form is very different from the juvenile form. Like the butterfly, we too have made a change from spiritual immaturity to spiritual maturity, from being confused to being confident. Physically, we may look the same, but spiritually and emotionally we are *completely* different. We are full-grown women ready to meet our Boaz and ready to serve God like never before!

The Caterpillar (The Old You)!

Caterpillars are known for being pests because they are voracious feeders, and in most cases, they eat more than their own body weight *daily*! Thus, being never satisfied, they are constantly in search of something to fulfill their appetites; they even eat their eggs after they lay them and they eat toxins. These toxins cause them to have venom in their hair, which can cause problems to anyone they encounter. The sight of a caterpillar is unattractive, wormlike, and can even be scary.

Before you began your man-kation, just like a caterpillar, you crawled on the ground (in the wilderness) searching for something and never being gratified. Various chapters in this book exposed our caterpillar life— we were broken-hearted, tricked by the enemy, living via our emotions, having a bad ego, hurting ourselves and others, and carrying so much baggage that we could not begin to even see the freedom that God gives through His love.

Many of us relied on our own insight and understanding because we tried to make things happen for ourselves and were *constantly* disappointed and confused.

This lifestyle caused us to destroy every relationship we had with men and other people because we longed for love, satisfaction, and peace in a place where none of those things exist. Your outer appearance may have been good, but on the inside, you were ugly and miserable. The wilderness was a volatile place that kept us defeated, deceived, and eventually would have caused death.

The Rest inside the Cocoon

When the caterpillar is in the process of forming its cocoon, it sheds its skin many times before the hard skin covers it. God showed me that is why our transformation can be so painful. We must be completely stripped of our old way of thinking, living, and acting. Killing your bad ego, dealing with past hurts, and taking responsibility for your actions is a lot to endure. The cocoon is God's garden, that *big* shoulder you need to lean on, to lift *all* the heavy burdens from the wilderness.

Once you gained the knowledge of godly love, your spirit began to rest in God's Love. He was waiting with open arms and those arms wrapped around you like a blanket (a cocoon). God kept you there to rescue you from the storms. He kept you there to reconstruct and improve your life! He separated you from everything and everyone in the wilderness so He could heal you on the inside for manifestation on the outside.

The world on the outside didn't see the change, but on the inside God was doing some miraculous things. Just like a cut on your finger, you don't see the healing until the scab (covering) forms on the skin. In the cocoon (our spiritual covering) of God, He completely wraps you in His spirit and protects you for His purpose. The longer you stay in His cocoon, the more you are *completely* restored from all the deep hurts and immersed in Him.

The cocoon stage of our spiritual maturity is the budding season to being a fruit-of-the-Spirit tree. When I was a child, my grandparents had different types of fruit trees on their land. I recall during the budding season the tree's buds didn't look like the fruit it would produce at all. The buds were tiny at first and turned different colors; I even tried eating some before time, and they tasted bitter.

Then as the weeks went by the buds would get bigger, and once they reached maturity, they looked perfect and tasted great! I used to wonder how the fruit grew because on the outside it looked like nothing was moving, but on the inside, there was definitely activity taking place.

We must think of our spiritual walk the same way. Even when we examine ourselves by looking at our current state of mind and current struggles, we must always *believe* that God is doing something on the inside of us. I started to take an evaluation of my progress (through journaling) during my man-kation, and I noticed that little things I used to do or think I stopped. Then God started dealing with bigger things. I tracked them, they took more time to change, but eventually I saw the change, and today I am still changing.

Keeping a journal during your man-kation is *very* important because it helps you to stay motivated and to stay on track. When you write something and date it, then go back weeks, months, or even years later, and you will *really* see the progress in your life. Please know that once you have a commitment to change, then change will take place, but it does not happen quickly; just keep pacing yourself and don't give up. I don't care how many times you drop the ball—stay in the race!

The cocoon keeps you cool through the heated moments in your life. When the fires flare up, stop, drop, and pray!

I'm talking about the fires of:

- Temptation to go back to the wilderness
- Doubting God's promises
- Acting on emotions/flesh
- Confusion

STOP what you're doing, thinking, or about to say. The cocoon will *not* allow you to go completely to the left anymore. Once you've come this far in God, there is a standard— a fence/barrier that he puts around you. There is no way to go back to the wilderness except to *completely* turn away from God!

DROP to your knees. Did you know that kneeling in prayer to God is a sign of humbleness? When we kneel, we put ourselves in a position to receive, because we block everything and everyone around us to hear from God. There were times when I was on my man-kation that I had to lay prostrate on the floor, face down begging for God to deliver me, help me, and change me!

PRAY until you hear from God. I would lie there and pray until I heard from Him, or until I felt peace in my spirit. Sometimes the only way to get back to your peace is to drop in God's arms and rest there in the cocoon of His love. There will be times when God will not quickly answer your prayers; you must enter His rest (Hebrews 11:4) and wait for His answer. God is so strong that He will not release you out of the cocoon until He knows you're ready.

While you're there enjoy His love, favor, presence, and bask in His glory. Just know that *all* things are working together for **your** good (Romans 8:28)!

The Beautiful Butterfly!

Butterflies are beautiful. They fly with elegance and are tranquil to watch. Did you know that butterflies have ultraviolet colorful patterns in their wings that we cannot see, but that can be seen by other butterflies? Many of the colorful ones also have dull-colored outer wings (that are visible when they are at resting). The color in their wings has multiple purposes.

Camouflage

Camouflage helps the butterfly blend into their environment to hide from predators. God will hide you from your enemies even when they think they have you cornered, God will protect you. This camouflage also helps you to blend in with other people to help save souls. Love is a universal language; when you demonstrate love, people will automatically be drawn to you. That is your opportunity to minister to them about a man named Jesus. Brag on Him and how He is the center of joy and peace in your life and tell your testimony of how He changed you.

Attracting and finding mates

Butterflies look for certain colors and patterns on the wings to find their mate! This goes back to Chapter 11, being a fruit-of-the-Spirit tree. Know that your Boaz will be looking for your patterns, and your spirit will vividly show your colors/fruit! Now that you are this beautiful butterfly, your radiance and loveliness is not to be taken lightly. Lady, you shine above all others and your confidence shows.

But ye are a chosen generation, a royal priesthood, an holy nation, a peculiar people; that ye should shew forth the praises of him who hath called you out of darkness into his marvelous light.

1 Peter 2:9

During your transformation from a caterpillar to a butterfly, you have learned some very insightful things about yourself and about God. You have also learned that your wilderness life is *over*, and you are walking in your God-given destiny. Godly people are *peculiar people* because we have God-given talents that fully equip us to amazing things.

Peculiar means distinctive in nature or character from others. Your distinctiveness is what separates you and makes you special. Many people that knew you before will say, "Oh you have changed," or "There's something different about you."

Man~kation Tip 27:
"Virtuous Women Walk in Dominion!"

Strength and dignity are her clothing and her position is strong and secure; she rejoices over the future [the latter day or time to come, knowing that she and her family are in readiness for it]!

Proverbs 31:25

It's Breakout Time!

The butterfly breaks out of the cocoon when it softens; when God decides He will release you to fly high with assurance. You are the blessed woman that God promised would inherit the earth and fullness of it (Psalms 37:11)! That means that everything in the earth belongs to you; now it's up to you to claim it and receive it. Power and dominion is in your hands because of the guarantee God has given you.

Virtue means conformity of one's life and conduct to moral and ethical principles; uprightness; rectitude. The only gift that we can give God is to live an upright life wholly and acceptable to Him. We already learned that He rewards those that diligently seek Him. So, we must always remind ourselves that the way we live our life is the only thing that we *can* give God.

He does not want us to be robots, but He does want us to be fully able to make good godly decisions based on His word through the wisdom He has given us. He has, does, and will always give us *more* than we could ever give Him!! Always keep that in mind, it will keep you humble when God promotes you!

Man~kation Tip 28: "Your Future is greater than your Past!"

For surely there is a latter end [a future and a reward], and your hope and expectation shall not be cut off.

Proverbs 23:18

Do you believe that your future is so much better than your past? After reading this book, I know that you do. I pray that this book has blessed you the same way it has blessed me! I still refer to different chapters to remind me of what God said. Your desire to have a man, husband, companion, lover, confidant, and lifetime partner is coming to pass sooner than you think. We serve a big God, so think big, and you will receive big things!

A new you with a new mind is what God created in you and you have taken the steps to the new life God promised. Everything is new—your hope, your peace, your vision, your attitude, everything. Now God is going to bless you in new ways because you have made it to the promised land; the land where God doesn't hold back anything, and every day is a new day full of expectation.

You own this land, so go and possess it; God said nothing will be cut off from you. Remember you can't do anything about your past, but your future belongs to you so embrace it!

Continue to keep going through the process!

Let's recap a few things to help you along the journey while on your man-kation to your butterfly transformation!

7 Steps to Victory while on Man-kation:

1. Stay Prayed & Praised up!

    - Pray *every day*! Prayer is our way of communicating with God. We ask for things (healing, deliverance, financial help, and wisdom) and give thanksgiving—thanking God for the things he has done, doing, and will do in our lives.

        Little Prayer equals Little Power, but "A lot of Prayer equals a lot of Power!" *

    - Listen to and sing praise and worship music. God inhabits the praises of his people; that is where he dwells. When we praise God in song and dance, that is fellowship with him. You will immediately feel the presence of God, which brings Joy, love, peace, and hope!

2. Read the Word Daily!

    - The word of God is your sword! When the enemy is on the attack and your feeling weak, say out loud

Philippians 4:13 "I can do all things through Christ which strengthens me." Reading the word builds your faith and helps to renew your mind.

3. Never doubt the Word!

- When you read the word, *never* doubt what God is saying. You must learn to trust God. By not doubting him/the Word, you are building trust. Trust will help you get through those tough times, knowing that God has your back!
- Remember, you are being processed for greatness; God's grace gives you the power to go through the fire/process without being burned. Stay connected.
- Hope is the rope that keeps you tied to belief! Just believe God's word is true!

4. Limit your conversations!

- Especially Men. Remember to walk in wisdom with them.
- Stop asking people for advice. *Only* accept the advice that lines up with the word of God!

- Spend more time meditating with God than on the phone with friends or online.

5. Realize emotions are *Not* your reality!

    - This is a huge one. As women we are emotional creatures, so emotions are a big part of our soul; they are necessary. However, we must— *must*— realize that emotions change just like the weather!
    - Do not be moved by your emotions but be moved by what God says!
    - Emotions *must* be put into perspective! Loneliness is not your reality. God is always with you! You are not a victim; you have the victory!

Yet amid all these things we are more than conquerors and gain a surpassing victory through Him Who loved us.

Romans 8:37

6. Take care of yourself

    - Continue to do things for you—pamper yourself, workout, eat right, go shopping (in moderation ladies) enjoy your life!

Remember, you're on a man-kation/vacation!

7. Sow good seed

    - Sowing a seed is giving, doing, or saying something that pleases God. When we sow these seeds, we will reap the *reward* from them. We cannot dictate when or how God will reward us; just know it's coming!

I am so excited about our promotion ladies and can't wait until God reveals our beauty to the world! We are spiritually blessed; we are a new creation and a representative of the Most High God of the universe! We are fresh, restored, and desire the best from God. All of God's promises are yes and *amen*!

I know that I have come full circle in this area of my life, because of the man-kation I *decided* to take. I had some bumps in the road, but God kept putting me back on track. I had some doubt, but God kept giving me confirmation. I was lost in the desires of my flesh, but I found the desires of God, transformed, and renewed—*the sky's the limit* for me and you!

Ladies, say this out loud:

> **I am FEARLESS because I move by what I BELIEVE and not what I see!**
>
> **I am WISE because it's the God in me!**
>
> **I am PHENOMENAL because that is who God created me to be!**

> **Let's fly high, Beautiful Butterflies!**

A Word of Thanks!

I want to first thank Jesus Christ, my Lord and Savior for giving me the inspiration and determination to write this book. Without Him I never would have had the courage or strength to do it!

I thank my grandmother, Mrs. Hazel Sheard. Even though you are 90 years old you still are a strong influence in my life! When I'm wrong you tell me, and when I'm right you would say something to encourage me to raise the bar! As your oldest grandchild, I have always felt that you have high expectations of me, and I thank you for setting the standard! I love the conversations we have, and I admire your strength and dignity. Thank you for supporting me with your prayers and wisdom. I recall asking you how I can live and be in good health, your answer was, "Don't smoke or drink, and *always* pay your tithes!"

To my mother, Doris White, I thank you, Mommy, for supporting me during the whole process of writing this book. When I was excited, you were excited, and when I needed to vent you would just listen. You have always been an encourager full of hope and grace. Your prayers and love have been very comforting to me!

My children, I thank you all for being the inspirations in my life to *never* give up! You are the reasons I strive to succeed in all the things I do! Your presence helps me to believe that God truly loves and favors me. I pray that I continue to lead by example the way God wants you to live. My prayer is that each of you keep God first in all that you do!

Thank you to my two sisters and my brother for your love and encouragement as well. As your big sister, I pray that I have helped to guide you during the different seasons of your lives. We share so many things, and I know God has something special planned for all of us!

To my extended families— the Sheard's, the Hatton's, the Wilson's, and the Robinson's— I love you all and feel so blessed to have such a huge family; too many to count but never forgotten in my prayers!

Meet the Author!

A. Renee Wilson was born in the Midwest to a middle-class family and reared there by her parents and grandparents. As the oldest child of her parents and the oldest grandchild of her maternal grandparents, she was raised to be a leader. She was brought up in the family's traditional Baptist church. As a youth she sang in various choirs and served on many different auxiliaries, which helped to lay the foundation for her Christian life.

Shortly after completing High School in Denver, Colorado, she moved to Atlanta, Georgia. For the past thirteen years, she has served at her local churches in various leadership roles—church administrator, pastor's assistant, prayer intercessor, missionary, and praise team member just to name a few. In 2008, she became an ordained minister of the gospel and since then has preached in the US as well as overseas.

Her international missionary work includes sponsoring orphans, ministering to prisoners, feeding the hungry, organizing rivals and donating clothes & shoes to the poor. She also organized sending thousands of supplies to the Haiti earthquake victims in 2009.

As a businesswoman, she has an entrepreneurial heart. She had a non-profit organization, ran her own janitorial business for many years, was a State of Georgia real estate license professional, and has been the founder and CEO of Perfecting Proverbs Publishing, LLC since 2013. She has a business degree in Human Resources and has been a corporate recruiter for many years.

She believes that *all* things are possible through Jesus Christ who strengthens you (Philippians 4:13). "God gives the vision he plants the seed, but it is up to you to go out by his grace and increase the seed!"